TRAINING YOUR
PET FERRET

Gerry Bucsis

Barbara Somerville

With Photographs by the Authors

BARRON'S

Dedication

This book is dedicated to Patch, the little furball who made it all possible.

Note of Warning

This book deals with the keeping and training of ferrets as pets. In working with these animals, you may occasionally sustain scratches or bites. Have such wounds treated by a doctor at once.

As a result of unhygienic living conditions ferrets can have mites and other external parasites, some of which can be transmitted to humans or to pet animals, including cats and dogs. Have the infested ferret treated by a veterinarian at once and go to the doctor yourself at the slightest suspicion that you may be harboring one of these pests. When buying a ferret, be sure to look for the signs of parasite infestation.

Ferrets must be watched very carefully during the necessary and regular exercise period in the house. To avoid life-threatening accidents, be particularly careful that your pet does not gnaw on any electrical wires.

All inquiries should be addressed to:
Barron's Educational Series, Inc.
250 Wireless Boulevard
Hauppauge, New York 11788

International Standard Book No. 0-7641-0093-9
Library of Congress Catalog Card No. 97-14721

Library of Congress Cataloging-in-Publication Data

Bucsis, Gerry.
    Training your pet ferret / Gerry Bucsis, Barbara Somerville.
        p.   cm.
    Includes bibliographical references (p. 76) and index.
    ISBN 0-7641-0093-9
    1. Ferrets as pets. 2. Ferrets as pets—Training.
I. Somerville, Barbara. II. Title.
SF459.F47B835   1997
636.9′76628—dc21   97-14721
                                 CIP

Printed in Hong Kong

9 8 7 6 5 4 3

Acknowledgments

Special thanks to:
- our long-suffering families for their support, understanding, and encouragement.
- our friends—Barb and Rica Hansen, Jane Panagabko, and Jodi Sawicki—who allowed their ferrets to be photographed.
- the following individuals and companies for their help and cooperation:
  - Contech Electronics, Inc.
  - Duke's Dog Fashions
  - Eight In One Pet Products, Inc.
  - Dave Franco, ADD Aquatics
  - Grannick's Bitter Apple, Co.
  - Dave McMahon, animal trainer
  - Mardel Laboratories
  - Marshall Pet Products, Inc.
  - Midwest Homes for Pets
  - Pet Value, Fonthill, ON
  - Qualex Canada Photofinishing
  - Real Animal Friends
  - Rolf C. Hagen Inc.
  - Shopper's Drug Mart, Niagara Falls, ON
  - "Super Pet" Pets International
  - John Valsamis, DVM
  - Katie Warden, Paulmac's
- our editor, Anna Damaskos, for expert assistance and unfailing good humor.
- The cover photo is courtesy of "Super Pet" Pets International; the inside front cover photo is by Norvia Behling; the stack of books pictured on the back cover are volumes of *COLLIER'S ENCYCLOPEDIA,* copyright © 1976 by P.F. Collier, Inc. Used by permission of the publisher; bottom photo on page viii, tent courtesy of Duke's Dog Fashions, Inc.; page 1, photo courtesy of "Super Pet" Pets International; photo on page 2, cage by Midwest Homes for Pets; photo on page 5, collar courtesy of Marshall Pet Products, Inc.; photo on page 7, carrier by Doskocil; photo on page 24, Hi-Corner litter pan courtesy of "Super Pet" Pets International; photo on page 35, sleep sack courtesy of Marshall Pet Products, Inc.; page 40, (top photo) ferret harnesses courtesy of Duke's Dog Fashions, Inc., Rolf C. Hagen, Inc., and Marshall Pet Products, Inc., (bottom photo) harness courtesy of Rolf C. Hagen, Inc.; page 50, photo courtesy of "Super Pet" Pets International; photo on page 51, Flying Cubby courtesy of Duke's Dog Fashions, Inc.; photo on page 54, red Carry-Go-Round courtesy of Duke's Dog Fashions, Inc.; photo on page 55, Carry-Go-Round courtesy of Duke's Dog Fashions, Inc.; photos on pages 70 and 72, Scat Mat courtesy of Contech Electronics, Inc.

Contents

Introduction

Can you handle a bundle of energy? Are you looking for a pet that will provide hours of fun for the whole family? Are you prepared for instant attention wherever you go? Congratulations! You've made the perfect choice. Ferrets are wonderful pets and will reward you with years of fun. They are playful, lovable, endearing, and intelligent.

They are, however, different from other house pets and need a special approach when it comes to training. Ferrets are much more inquisitive and resourceful than the average cat or dog. They are constantly on the go when awake and can get into things that Tabby wouldn't even dream of! If you go out and leave your cat alone, Tabby will snooze on the sofa. If you leave your ferret on the loose, the little rascal will ransack the kitchen cupboards.

And, if you think your ferret can be trained like Fido, think again. Fido will be perfectly happy to perform his party tricks for a "Good boy, well done!" Praise alone satisfies man's best friend, but it won't register with your ferret.

So, how do you train this free-roaming, curious bundle of energy? You won't find ferret obedience classes in the Yellow Pages. None of the available ferret care guides offers a complete training program—they offer only sporadic advice. Consequently, owners have had to glean information from a variety of sources such as veterinarians, other owners, ferret organizations, and friendly pet shop staff. Often, training has been a matter of trial and error (mostly error!).

But now there is *Training Your Pet Ferret*—all *you* ever wanted to know about training your ferret but didn't know who to ask. This is *not* a general care guide. There are excellent books available that provide detailed information about choosing a ferret, as well as advice on health care, grooming, and breeding. In fact, every ferret owner should have a quality care guide on hand.

Training Your Pet Ferret is a training guide. In a step-by-step approach, this book outlines specific methods for teaching and reinforcing positive behavior in your ferret. It also makes suggestions on how to tackle negative behavior: in short, the A to Z of ferret training.

So now it's up to you. Have realistic expectations for your pet. Set aside some time each day for practice. Be consistent. But most importantly, have FUN!

"I'm ready for action. Are you?"

A tent full of ferret fun.

Chapter One
First Things First: Preparations

Before training, there's work to be done

Now that you've made the big decision to buy a ferret, you probably want to rush right out to the pet shop and bring one home. But stop! You want to start off on the right foot, don't you? After all, the little guy will be with you for many years. Taking time to prepare adequately beforehand will be time well spent. The good news is that you won't have to break the bank for the few items you need to get started. First on your list should be home sweet home.

A ferret's house is his castle

Your ferret's cage has to be his haven, a retreat where he feels safe and secure. This is where he'll play when you're out during the day. This is where he'll most likely crash between bouts of furious activity. This is where he needs to be for his own safety when you're sleeping. Left to roam unsupervised, he can get into too much mischief.

There are several types of suitable housing. A large wire cage is an excellent choice. It will give your ferret a good window on the world, letting him see what's going on

A wire cage is a good choice for your ferret.

There's lots of room for exercise and play in a Ferret Playpen.

away from fringes or rubber backing, please!

Less desirable are the extra-large dog crates used for air travel—they will limit your ferret's view too much. And stay away from aquariums. They may look good and be within your price range, but ventilation and overheating can be a problem, especially in the summer.

What you buy will depend upon your budget and the amount of space you have available, but try to choose something that will give your pet plenty of room. By the time you put the bowls, the bedding, the litter box, and the toys together, be sure there's room for your ferret!

around him. You can jazz up the interior decor by hanging up playthings, tubes, and hammocks for a more ferret-friendly environment. Multistory cages with wire ladders and/or plastic platforms will need some modification. Carpet the wire ladders or slip them into hockey socks. Platforms should be made soft and safe with fleecy covers or carpet. Are you in the market for luxury real estate? Large Ferret Condos are spacious and offer upscale comfort. Are you a do-it-yourselfer? Instructions for homemade cages can be found in general ferret care books. Ferret feet and wire flooring don't go together, so any of these choices can be made comfy with a piece of linoleum or a washable carpet mat on the floor. Stay

Location, location, location

Find a good spot in your house for the cage and leave it there. Animals become confused if they're constantly being moved. How would you like to find your bed in the kitchen one night and in the laundry room the next? Ferrets snooze an average of 14 hours a day. They're dead to the world when they sleep, so the spot you choose for the cage doesn't have to be a quiet one. In fact, it's preferable to locate it in a busy area of the house. Ferrets are sociable and will want to be where the action is. Just make sure to keep the cage out of direct sunlight and away from heating vents. Heat can be harmful to fur-coated ferrets.

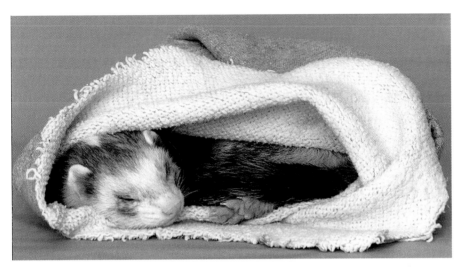

Bedding basics

For sleeping, ferrets like to burrow into soft bedding. Ready-made ferret tubes and sleep sacks are cozy and convenient. But there's no need to purchase anything special. Just look around your house. You'll be surprised what you can come up with. Try towels, cut-off sweatpant legs, flannel pajamas, hockey socks, old sweatshirts, or blankets. Watch out for anything detachable that could be chewed off and swallowed. No hooks, snaps, buttons, beads, elastic, or plastic caps. Nix anything that has small holes because your ferret could crawl through them and get stuck. Find plenty of washable bedding that can be popped in the washer when it starts to get that familiar ferret fragrance.

Occasionally a baby ferret, called a kit, might chew his cloth bedding. A swallowed piece can cause intestinal blockage. So, if your ferret is a material muncher, try a small cardboard box or a snooze tube instead.

Never use cedar chips or shavings as bedding. A naturally occurring chemical in the cedar can cause respiratory problems in small animals. Shredded newspapers are a ferret favorite, but the inks used today have a tendency to rub off. Do you really want your ferret licking yesterday's headlines off his fur?

A passing look at litter

Every cage's floor plan should include space for a litter box. Have one ready and waiting for your new pet because he won't be able to wait until you run out and find one. The ins and outs of the litter box are covered in Chapter 6.

Food for thought— a square meal

After you've set your ferret's house in order, the next important consideration is his food. If you don't provide proper nutrition for your pet, he can stuff himself and still starve. Ferrets need high-quality dry food. The protein content must be at least thirty-two percent, most of which should be animal protein. The fat content should be between twenty and thirty percent.

These requirements are met in specially formulated ferret foods such as Eight In One Ferret Ultra-Blend, Hagen Ferret Diet, Marshall Premium Ferret Diet, Path Valley Farm Ferret Food, or Totally Ferret.

High-quality dry kitten or cat foods like Iams or Science Diet will also meet your pet's nutritional needs. For the finicky eater, try a custom blend of different brands or types. Canned ferret food is nutritionally balanced, but, to keep teeth and gums healthy, it should be used in conjunction with dry food. Don't use dog food or puppy chow and stay away from bargain basement cat or kitten foods. From a nutritional standpoint, they won't fit the bill. If you have doubts about a particular product, check with your veterinarian.

What goes in must come out. And in a ferret's case, the job gets done quickly! A ferret eats often and digests food in three to four hours. So food and fresh water must be available at all times in the cage and in the play area for eating on the run.

Battening down the bowls

Food flying, water sloshing, ferret clucking—the food-flippin' ferret strikes again! Dragging dishes, upending bowls, scattering food, and soaking bedding—what fun (for the ferret, that is)!

How can you prevent a movable feast? Invest in sturdy, tip-proof bowls. The best bets are heavy, medium-sized crockery bowls or man-made marble dishes. The trick is to find something heavy that your ferret can't nudge, drag, or flip with his nose, mouth, or paws.

To prevent tipping, drill holes in plastic clip-on bowls . . .

. . . and attach them to the cage wire.

When choosing bowls that attach to the cage, look for the type where the bowls themselves, rather than the frames, are secured to the wire. Crock Loc is an example of what you want. These dishes fasten to the cage and lock in place. They are easily removed for cleaning and refilling. A J-feeder is also tip-proof and has the added advantage of holding more food.

Alternatively, you can modify common plastic clip-on bowls. Using two stainless steel bolts, two wing nuts, and a small, stainless steel plate with predrilled holes, secure each bowl to the cage as illustrated in the photographs on page 4.

Water bottles attached to the cage won't tip. But find one that doesn't drip, unless, of course, your pet has his rubber boots handy! Here's another point to remember—water bottles won't work if your kit hasn't mastered the art of sipping. You might have to teach him how it's done by putting his mouth to the water tube.

Ring around the collar

A collar with a small bell attached needs to be on your shopping list. In fact, you might as well get two—one and a spare. It's not the collar that's so important; it's the bell. Any ferret, big or small, can whisk around the house in almost total

silence. A bell will allow you to keep track of your pet so that you won't spend half your life looking for him. Also, when you know where he is, you'll be less likely to step on him.

If (heaven forbid!) your pet ever escapes to the great outdoors, a bell will increase your chances of finding him a hundredfold, as will a tiny I.D. tag. If you can't find an I.D. tag small enough, check with your local jewelry store about getting his bell engraved with your telephone number or use a hand engraver to do it yourself.

Use a ferret collar or kitten collar, it doesn't matter which, as long as there's a bell attached. If you can find a collar with some stretch or a

A small bell on his collar will help you keep track of your ferret.

break-away safety feature, all the better. It will help prevent choking if your tireless explorer gets hooked on a piece of furniture.

Given half a chance, little Houdini will slip out of his collar, so make sure that it's snug but not too tight. Check the fit periodically. Ferrets expand on their own, collars don't! Some ferrets take to a collar easily; others fight it tooth and nail and squirm out at every opportunity. What should you do with the non-conformist? Persevere. Make the collar just a teensy bit tighter. Then, every time he slips it off, put it back on and give him a treat. If he loses it, put on the spare immediately and spare yourself a lost ferret.

The carrot and the stick

Because training starts the very minute you pick up your pet, you'll want to have two valuable training aids on hand before bringing him home.

The first of these is Ferretone, a coat and vitamin supplement. Because most ferrets adore Ferretone, it will be the carrot you dangle in front of your pet's nose to encourage and reinforce good behavior. Order it from your pet store if it's not readily available in your area.

Linatone is an acceptable substitute. However, the recommended daily allowance of three to five drops does not stretch very far for training rewards. Don't use both Ferretone and Linatone on the same day. A double dose of vitamins is too much of a good thing. Stick to one and follow the label directions carefully.

The second item is Bitter Apple spray. It's the only type of corrective stick to use with your pet, as physical force is never recommended in disciplining ferrets. Bitter Apple works wonders. It discourages nipping, curbs chewing, and can be very helpful when rehabilitating a problem ferret. The spray is not harmful; ferrets just hate the taste.

Vetting the vets

There's one last step before you're ready to go. Call around until you find a veterinarian who is knowledgeable about and experienced with ferrets. Don't be afraid to ask questions. You'll need to arrange for an initial checkup and for canine distemper and rabies shots. Ask about neutering or spaying your pet if this hasn't already been done. Neutering a male reduces odor and results in a ferret with a quieter disposition. Females *must* be spayed if not kept for breeding. Otherwise, they go into prolonged heat, which results in life-threatening health problems. The pros and cons of de-scenting, if not done already, can also be discussed with the veterinarian. Regular health checks are necessary for your pet's well-being. Keep in mind that a healthy ferret is a happy ferret.

Chapter Two
Bonding with Your Buddy

Getting to know you

When the pre-pet preparations are taken care of, you'll be ready for what really counts—bonding with your buddy. Bonding is all about building trust. It's about you and your ferret getting to know and love one another. Whether you choose a tiny kit or adopt an adult, bonding begins with homecoming.

Homecoming

The great moment has arrived! It's time to bring home the new addition to the family. This may well be the second move for your kit— first from the mother to the pet shop and then from the pet shop to your house. She may even have had a stopover with a distributor. So, you'll want to make this move as agreeable as possible.

For the ride home, buy a travel carrier or find a small box that you can take with you to the pet shop, shelter, or breeder. Line it with the soft bedding you intend to use in the cage. Your pet will feel more secure in the confined space of the box than she would on a passenger's lap, and the bedding will give her a place to hide. She won't appreciate loud music and poking fingers, but do reassure her by speaking softly.

As soon as you get home, gently place your ferret in her new cage. The sights, sounds, and smells of your house may be very frightening for her. *You* might be anxious to play with your baby or show her to

A travel carrier keeps Farley safe on the way to his new home.

friends and neighbors. *She* will be overwhelmed. Leave her alone for a few hours to adjust to this strange, new environment. Fresh food, water, and toys will help her feel at home. Don't worry if your kit starts scratching frantically to escape. She'll settle down after a while, curl up, and sleep. When she wakes up, the fun begins!

To have is to hold

When the new arrival's up and about and has had a good sniff around her new quarters, it's time for handling session number one. You don't want to startle her, so speak quietly as you pick her up. Cradling the newcomer in your arms, stroke her fur, rub her ears, and scratch her under the chin. Massage those hind legs and tickle that tummy. Brush her with a cat brush as you whisper sweet nothings in her ear.

Keep in mind that a kit is a baby with lots of energy. She may not want to be handled at first, so be prepared for wriggling and jumping. Be careful, don't drop her, but handle her anyway. Don't put her down as soon as she starts wriggling. Hold her a little bit longer to show who's boss. After all, who's training whom?

Your ferret needs to learn that being held is enjoyable. It's amazing how a few licks of Ferretone can help get this message across. So, when she's in angelic mode, cuddling close, give her a reward for good behavior.

How often is enough?

That's it for your first handling session. There wasn't much to it, was there? It's a snap from here on in. Just repeat the handling over and over, and over and over, and over and over, and—get the point?

So, how often is enough? Try to get in as many short socializing sessions per day as possible. Even five minutes at a time is fine. In fact, many short sessions are better than a few marathon ones. Are you busy at work or school all day? Try to find time for your ferret before going out in the mornings and as soon as you get home. Just don't expect a kit who's caged all day to cooperate miraculously at supper time!

The best way to bond with your new ferret is to handle her often—very often. *The more frequently you handle your kit, the more loving she will be as an adult.* The same holds true if you've adopted an older ferret. Frequent handling is the key to success.

Rebel on the run

If you have a little rebel with ideas of her own—mainly run, run, run—you can make things easy on yourself. Get out the secret weapon you have on hand—Ferretone! This is wonderful stuff. A drop or two on a plastic spoon will have her licking her lips. She'll soon stop struggling

Taz plays hard to get— bring out the Ferretone!

when she realizes that being held equals a goodie.

Here's another trick to keep up your sleeve for those times when the kit won't cooperate. It's much easier to handle a full ferret. A hungry one will be more interested in visiting her food bowl than visiting with you.

Sometimes, though, there might be a legitimate reason for a squirmy ferret. The wiggles could mean she needs exercise. Several daily workouts in a restricted area are essential. See Chapters 4 and 5.

If she's extremely squirmy, perhaps she needs to use the litter box *right now*. Excessive fidgeting is universal ferret body language for "I gotta go!" Pop her back into the cage and try handling her again later.

All in the family

Make handling your ferret a family affair. From Junior to Gramps, get everyone in on the act. Just don't let everybody grab for her at once. Take a low-key approach. The newcomer should feel safe and secure, not scared out of her wits.

Do kids and ferrets mix? Some veterinarians don't recommend ferrets as pets for small children. Check with your veterinarian if you have concerns. Young children should not be around a ferret, or any animal, without adult supervision. Older children need instruction on proper handling and care.

It's only natural for kids to want to hold and hug a new pet. Unfortunately, a baby ferret might have something else in mind, namely a fast getaway. You need to step in as the bonding coach. Pick a time when the kit is cooperative. Bring out the Ferretone. Then sit your child down with the ferret for a short hold and treat session. This is the way to go till kid and kit get to be best buddies.

. . . and from Justin.

Chapter Three
Nipping Is a No-No

Nip it in the bud

Most kits are sweet and snugly, good-natured and gentle. They are owner-friendly from day one. Why then are others a bit nippy? In the litter, rough and tumble is the name of the game. Chasing, batting, swatting, darting, bounding, rolling, wrestling, and nipping are all part of playtime. And it may not occur to your kit to stop the roughhousing just because his address has changed.

Do you have a little hooligan on your hands? You'll have to teach him to mind his manners. Don't let your pet get away with any nipping at all. Every time he nips, hold him about a foot from your face, look him straight in the eye and say a short, sharp "NO!" If this doesn't register, reinforce the "NO!" with a *light* flick on the nose.

A variation on this approach involves the use of a small ferret chew bone. Whenever your kit nips, say a firm "NO!" and give him the bone to chew. This redirects the negative behavior (nipping) to an acceptable alternative (the chew bone). Or, you can mimic Mama Fer-ret. Hold him by the scruff of the neck and give him a *little* shake. Add a hiss or two and you'll be the perfect overbearing parent.

What about the incorrigible kit who's not getting the no-nip message? Don't despair. Instead of wringing your hands, spray them with Bitter Apple. Your terrible tasting fingers will soon teach your pet that nipping is a no-no.

Treat your kit kindly when you're teaching him to mind his manners. Never point an angry finger at him and avoid using his name when he's being disciplined. In all training, your pet needs to connect his name with pleasantries.

Twinkle toes

It's no secret that ferrets love to get wound up when they play. When your bundle of energy is bouncing around, ping-ponging back and forth, don't be surprised if your toes become a target—especially toes in panty hose. Toes are just too tantalizing for a ferret to ignore. But toe nipping is something *you* can't ignore. The Ferret Fandango may seem like fun when he's a kit, but it won't be so cute when he's an adult.

When your kit does a nip and run or takes a shine to your socks, pick him up and say a firm "NO!" Then redirect his energy to another fun activity. If he has a real foot fetish, whip out the Bitter Apple spray and spritz those tootsies (yours, not his!). The bitter taste should quickly turn him off your toes. If there are any relapses, spray again.

Don't ever play footsies with your ferret. Wiggling your toes under his nose will just confuse him. He won't know when a toe attack is okay and when it's not.

Rehab hints

Are you one of the admirable owners giving an adult adoptee a second chance? Good for you! The rewards can be heartwarming. Many ferrets adjust to a new home with enthusiasm and soon become part of the family. For others, the road is a little rockier. Ferrets who have been neglected or mistreated may nip or even bite out of fear. Kind-ness, patience, and understanding are in order here. Your aim is to build trust, but this can be difficult with a fearful ferret. He's afraid, so he bites you; you're afraid, so you won't handle him. How do you break this cycle and begin bonding?

Find a sturdy pair of garden gloves and spray them liberally with Bitter Apple. Wear a long-sleeved shirt and spray the sleeves as well. Now you'll be able to hold the ferret and give him the attention he needs. Handle him frequently for short periods and follow the instructions for bonding in Chapter 2. This way, he'll begin to associate you with good things—brushing, stroking, talking gently, getting treats. Keep discipline to a minimum and reward him generously for good behavior. If he becomes truly unmanageable, time out in the cage can help him calm down.

It could take weeks for the newcomer to respond. Building trust takes time, but hang in there. After a while you'll be able to give up the gloves and just spray your hands. The final step occurs when trust triumphs and the Bitter Apple goes back on the shelf.

Chapter Four
Safe and Sound

Safety first

Your ferret is a unique pet with somewhat eccentric tastes. Run-of-the-mill catnip or milkbones are not for her, thank you! A Lysol cocktail or rubber appetizer is more up her alley. And forget that cozy spot in front of the fire. Dark, claustrophobic spaces are what attract your furry friend.

It's because ferrets eat unusual things and get into unusual places that ferret-proofing is absolutely essential. Your mission is simple—make the space safe. Crawl around on your hands and knees in every room your pet will roam and ask yourself the following questions— Can she eat it? Can she drink it? Can she open it? Can she get into it? Can she get stuck in it? Can she escape from it?

Take the house tour in this chapter. You'll learn to look at your home from a ferret's point of view and size up potential hazards. You'll also get practical ferret-proofing solutions. Read through every section in this chapter and zero in on whatever applies to your place.

A clean sweep in the kitchen

Take one ferret, pop her into the average kitchen, look the other way, and you'll have a recipe for disaster. Wherever she turns, there's temptation. Soap, dishwashing detergent, cleansers, plant sprays—all these forbidden fruits will draw her like a magnet. That's no big problem, you might think—just stow the stuff in the cupboards. Wrong! You haven't seen anything until you've seen ferret paws pry open a door or a drawer. An easy way to take care of this problem is to store everything in seal-tight containers. Another option is to install baby locks. But beware. Not all childproof locks are ferret-proof. Tot-Loks, however, are ideal. Good for both cupboards and drawers, these magnetic locks will stymie even the most determined ferret.

Rubber is *the* ferret favorite, so keep sink mats, sink stoppers, and rubber gloves out of reach. Check also for bumpers on cabinet or refrigerator doors. Anything made of sponge also has a fatal attraction for

Your ferret's svelte and sinuous body (the kind you've always dreamed of) allows her to slink behind, between, and beneath the stove, the fridge, the dishwasher, and the cupboard kickboards. To keep her out of harm's way, arm yourself with sturdy cardboard and duct tape. Block off any spaces larger than one inch across by cutting cardboard to fit and anchoring it with tape. For larger spaces, fold the cardboard and wedge it into place.

A guest in the living room?

Grab a cup of coffee, head for the living room, and have a good look around. Ask yourself whether you want your ferret in here. If not, French doors, folding doors, or louvered doors could be the answer. Do you need a cheaper and less permanent solution? On the left inside door frame, make a track by attaching two thin strips of wood a half-inch apart. Do the same on the right side. Stain or paint the tracks to match the woodwork, then slot in a piece of plexiglass. Voila! Limited admission.

But, if she's going to be welcome, take a few precautions *before* letting her loose. Move those knickknacks off the tables before she does and keep drinks out of reach. If your kit shows an interest in lamp cords, smear them with Bitter Apple cream (the cream lasts longer than the

Ferrets are a whiz at getting into cupboards and drawers.

your ferret. Keep all sponges in closed margarine tubs and store mops with their heads up, not down at ferret level.

Does your little scamp like rifling through the garbage? A pedal bin or step-on trash can will prevent ferret foraging. To stop a nosy kit from playing in the oven storage drawer, tape the drawer shut. Also tape the refrigerator kickplate so she can't get at the motor, coils, and insulation.

spray). And watch out for hot water radiators. Little heads can get stuck in little places.

Before you go flopping on the sofa to catch forty winks, take a quick look under the cushions. A ferret couch potato could be hogging the spot already. Speaking of the sofa, your ferret might pry back the gauzy material underneath so she can crawl inside. What a great hidey hole for snoozing or caching loot! If your pet tries this trick, staple the material back to the frame and dab it with Bitter Apple cream. If she's persistent and ignores your pleas, you may have to resort to stapling small-holed chicken wire across the underside. Don't fret. No one but your ferret will see it anyway! And it's much better than having a stowaway in your sofa.

An enterprising ferret, looking for adventure, might pull out a heating vent and crawl into the duct work. Warning! Warning! She could get lost or hurt. Spare yourself the hassle; check your vent covers. Some have tabs on the sides that can be pried out with a screwdriver to ensure a tighter fit. Others will have to be screwed to the floor.

Focus on the family room

Family room frolics can be fast and furious with a ferret around. But before the fun begins, ferret-proof, ferret-proof, ferret-proof.

Ferrets can squeeze into small spaces—be sure to block off any trouble spots.

At the top of the list is the reclining chair. Ferrets like to climb inside these chairs and can get stuck or crushed in the mechanism. Do you know where Pippi's sleeping when you put your feet up for a rest? Because these chairs are a major cause of injury to ferrets, most books recommend getting rid of them. But if Mom won't part with her favorite lounger, a cheap and easy solution is to disable the chair by doctoring the footrest and the reclining back.

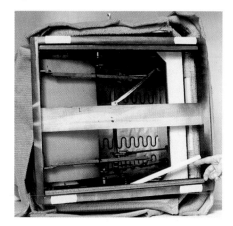

Disable your recliner with strong rope or wooden dowels.

First, disable the footrest. If there's a side lever, remove it. Where there's a push button, upend the chair and disconnect the cable that operates the footrest. When all else fails, take strong rope or clothesline and tie the metal footrest supports to an immovable part of the chair frame.

Next, inactivate the reclining back. Upend the chair and look for the two large wing nuts that control the reclining mechanism. Tighten these as much as possible. For chairs with sliding tracks, cut two wooden dowels or slats and insert one in each track.

Lastly, stuff any openings around the bottom of the now non-recliner with cardboard and tape or with rolled chicken wire. Your ferret can get stuck even in a disabled mechanism.

A rocking recliner is a bigger safety headache yet. Rockers crush ferrets. So after you've fixed the footrest and the back, you must stop the rocking motion. Shove a wooden wedge under the back and

Wooden wedges prevent rocking recliners from rocking.

front of each rocker and secure it with duct tape. Regular rocking chairs should be relocated to a ferret-free zone.

If you have an oddball chair that's in a class of its own or you don't trust your fix-it skills, trot on down to your friendly furniture store and ask the service person for advice. Test any adjustments you make to ensure that you no longer have a recliner or a rocking recliner. Your ferret's worth the sacrifice!

With sofa beds, not only is the mechanism a concern, Pippi can also crawl into the folded mattress and get stuck, sat on, or smothered. What's the solution? Keep her out by blocking off the bottom. Open up the bed and line the inside edges of the sofa frame with lengths of scrap 2×4-inch wood, cut or pieced to fit. In some spots where wood won't fit, cardboard and duct tape will.

Do you like to unwind with music or watch TV after a long day? Keep an eye on headphones and remote controls or else they could wind up in Pippi's stockpile. And watch out for the stereo speakers. Some ferrets can pop off the front panels in no time flat and wreak havoc on those woofers and tweeters. Take steps to protect your investment. Small speakers can be put up high or on pedestals, but large floor speakers are a different matter—they don't fit on most book shelves! You could keep your music critic out of the room. Or, you can place semicircular Scat Mats around the speakers. This is a surefire solution as long as the mats are secured to the floor with one-inch wide masking tape. See Chapter 15 for the scoop on Scat Mats.

Foam or rubber weather stripping around windows and doors can be quite appetizing. Here's another job for Bitter Apple spray or cream. And last but not least, are there any doors to the outside in the room? Be absolutely certain that *everyone* in the family closes *every* door, *every* time, or Pippi will go AWOL.

Rec room review

Anyone for ping-pong? Your ferret will be happy to retrieve the balls. She'll also be happy to nibble the rubber off your ping-pong paddles. So watch where you set them down. If pool is your pastime, keep an eye on your cue. Your ferret will have her eye on the rubber tip. Be alert and check any games for small pieces of rubber or foam that could cause internal blockage if swallowed.

Is the rec room the hobby center of the house? Wine makers, store plastic tubing and corks well out of reach. Crafters, safeguard your supplies. Model enthusiasts, keep your kits out of your kits. Artists, guard those gum erasers. Get the picture?

If you have retired an elderly sofa or chair to the rec room, inspect all seams for leaks. Some ferrets eat shredded foam. You can repair a torn seam with heavy quilting thread and a curved upholstery needle, or try using duct tape. It sticks to almost anything. If the underside of the furniture has seen better days, use the chicken wire solution (see page 15) or take off the furniture's legs.

Overhauling the office

Whether you have a fully equipped home office or make do with a desk in the corner, you'll have your furry friend nosing around. No, she's not after your official secrets. What she really wants are those ferret favorites—rubber bands, erasers, and stick tack. Other tasty tidbits are

Rearranging the files ferret-style.

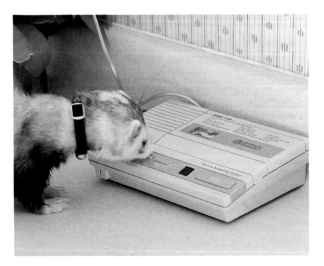

calculator buttons and plastic sleeves for computer disks. And have you ever noticed those little protective pads under lamps, desk organizers, telephones, and so on? These cork or rubber bumpers are bad news for tiny tummies.

While you're getting into your hard drive, your pet will be getting into the file cabinet (keep it closed) and the wastebasket (get one with a lid) and up into the desk drawers from behind (use cardboard and duct tape to close any openings). Ferrets also like to reprogram the answering machine. So if you've missed any messages, check with your ferret!

Bed and bath

When it comes to the bedroom, don't be caught napping, or you could open your sock drawer and find more than you bargained for!

Better ferret-proof either your drawers or your dressers.

Does your ferret treat your box springs as a safety deposit box? By tearing away a small corner of the gauze covering, she can get inside and cache her valuables—or yours. You can put a stop to this the same way you took care of the sofa in the living room.

A child's bedroom should be out of bounds. A million and one things in it are ferret unfriendly. Can you guarantee that dinky car wheels, super balls, balloons, ear plugs, play clay, foam, flip-flops, and so on are always out of reach?

Before your buddy makes whoopee in the bathroom, stash all cotton balls and swabs, sponges, and feminine hygiene products. Lock up the Lysol and keep the soap out of sight. After your Saturday morning cleaning blitz, don't leave the toilet brush lying around; your ferret will lap up the leftover cleanser. Put away the brush holder, too. Drippings that pool in the bottom can be tempting. Pull the plug after your bath—ferrets can climb into the tub. And watch your step! Towels, clothes, and throw rugs on the floor could be concealing a kit.

Don't forget to plug any openings around the plumbing pipes with stainless steel pot scrubbers (not the steel wool variety), chicken wire, Polyfilla, or cardboard and duct tape. You don't want your ferret wandering around in your walls or paying unscheduled visits to the next apartment.

Keep the dehumidifier ferret free with . . .

Down to the basement

If you let your ferret run about in the cellar, you could be singing the basement blues. Singed whiskers won't be Pippi's only problem if she's caught napping in the furnace or under the hot water tank. Don't let her near either. The furnace area should be off limits.

Is your basement on the damp side with a dehumidifier as part of the decor? A resourceful ferret can pull out the water container and help herself to a drink—and another and another and another, until she gets sick. Thwart her efforts with tape or Velcro.

Do you keep tripping over sports equipment drying in the basement? When checking your gear for mildew, check it also for foam, rubber, or sponge. Ferrets will tackle tennis shoe insoles, rubber squash balls, soccer shin guards, baseball shoe cleats, and the padding in football and hockey gear. You could stuff the equipment into a sports bag, but be aware that unzipping zippers is an uncanny ferret talent.

. . . Velcro or tape.

19

clamp, tape, or bolt it securely in place. And always sift through the laundry carefully—ferrets are strictly "hand wash and towel dry."

Safety on the stairway

When you're racing up or down stairs, yield to fast-moving ferrets overtaking from behind or changing lanes in front. Accidents can happen. Your ferret darts back and forth so quickly, it's easy for her to be trampled underfoot. The best way to avoid serious injury is to let her go ahead or carry her.

The laundry room

It's probably safer to keep your ferret out of the laundry room altogether. It's not just the detergent, fabric softener, stain removers and bleach she can get at. She might sneak under the washer and nibble the drive belts, chew through the dryer vent and crawl outside, or get tossed into the wash when snoozing in the dirty clothes.

If the laundry room can't be closed off, ferret-proof it. Board up any openings. Replace flexible vinyl or aluminum/polyester dryer venting with either rigid aluminum or flexible compressed aluminum venting and

All done!

Now that you're completely overwhelmed by what you've just read, take heart. Every house and ferret is different. There's not much chance that everything mentioned in this chapter will apply to your situation. Ferret-proofing may seem like work, but the suggested solutions don't involve a lot of time or money. And after all, isn't it worth a little effort to keep your ferret safe and sound?

Chapter Five

Exploring the Environment

Curious critters

To say that your ferret is inquisitive is an understatement. When it comes to curiosity, a ferret beats a cat hands down. He's the Sherlock Holmes of the animal kingdom, a true detective who'll peer, pry, and probe into every hole and corner. How do you think the term *ferret out* came about?

You don't have to train your ferret to investigate his environment. Exploration is basic to his nature. He'll do it automatically and enthusiastically. But you will have a job to do. You'll need to direct and supervise his activities and, of course, to ferret-proof each room before he has access to it. (You did read Chapter 4, didn't you?)

Decisions, decisions

Before you set your super sleuth loose, you'll have to give some thought to his field of operation.

Some ferrets are kept mainly in their cages and let out for two or three lengthy exercise periods per day. Others are allowed out of their cages all the time. Most fall somewhere in between. Some ferrets have one room designated as an exercise and play area, while others have full run of the house or apartment. Again, most fall somewhere in between. What's the best way to go for you and your pet? How much freedom and how much territory will he be allowed?

To help you decide, here's a list of questions to ask yourself. How much time do you have to spend supervising your ferret's antics? How big is your house or apartment? What is the layout of your living space? How easy is it to keep your ferret out of certain rooms? How determined is your pet? How rambunctious is he? How house-friendly is he? How tolerant are you? How many litter boxes are you willing to clean? And, most importantly, can you guarantee his safety?

There are no right or wrong answers. Every household is different.

Every ferret is different. What you decide will be based on your individual circumstances. And your decision needn't be written in stone. You may want to reevaluate when you and your ferret know each other better. Keep in mind, though, that a ferret is a companion pet, not a cage animal.

However much freedom you allow him, your pet should always be in his cage when you are sleeping or out of the house. Otherwise, his safety will be seriously compromised. Remember the old saying, "Curiosity killed the cat"? Well, your ferret doesn't have nine lives like a cat.

Limiting turf

So how do you get off to a good start when introducing Sherlock to his new surroundings? "Elementary, my dear Watson!" Limit his turf. A small area is less overwhelming and gives him a chance to explore safely. It gives you more control and the opportunity to see what he can get into. This is when you find out if you paid attention to Chapter 4.

If your ferret is to be confined to a one-room headquarters, his turf is limited automatically. If he'll eventually roam your whole house, you need to restrict his investigations to one room at first. Pick a small room or block off part of a large one.

The investigator

Wait until your ferret has wakened and used the litter box in his cage before his first foray. Speaking softly, pick him up gently and cuddle him. Then, take him over to the space you've designated as the first exploration site. Sit down (at floor level if possible), let him loose, and watch carefully.

Once he gets a whiff of freedom, Sherlock will start to case the joint—prying into cupboards, peering under furniture, seeking out adventure. He'll sniff each and every square inch, usually following the perimeter of the area first. Every nook and cranny will get the once over, even the twice or thrice over! You might want to put a few toys in the area, but he probably won't be interested until he's finished exploring this uncharted territory. In fact, don't try to distract him from his mission. Let him explore to his heart's content. Remember that the whole idea of this exercise is to get your pet accustomed to his new environment. You might want to play, but he will want to snoop.

The super sleuth nosing around his new surroundings.

If this is a place where you plan to keep a litter box, be sure to introduce him to it right away. Even if he just used the pan in his cage, he needs to know where this one is. If this is not an area where you plan to have a litter box, put him back in his cage every twenty to thirty minutes for a potty break.

Expanding horizons

For a few days or longer, stick to the same old scene and the same old routine. Let Sherlock get completely comfortable with the territory before increasing his play area. Then, gradually over weeks or months, expand his range one room at a time. In each new room, give your little gumshoe a chance to check out the joint under your watchful eye. You may decide that some places in the house aren't appropriate for your nosy critter. And that's okay.

On guard

As a responsible ferret owner, you always have to keep an eye open for calamities waiting to happen. You never know when someone could leave an outside door open or drop a cotton ball or forget to close a cupboard. For you, the case is never closed. Like the faithful Watson, you've got to be Sherlock's right-hand man, watching out for his well-being.

Chapter Six
Poop Goes the Weasel

Litter training— fact or fiction?

Is your little furball a potty pro, semi-pro, veteran, or rookie? Will the accidents stop this year, next year, sometime, never? What *are* the facts about litter training ferrets? The good news is that, yes, your ferret can be trained to use a litter pan. The not so good news is that most will have the occasional accident. People tend to judge litter pan success by cat standards. However, you have a ferret for a pet, not a cat. And ferret standards aren't always as accurate. A lot depends upon the individual ferret, how much time she spends in her cage, how much of

the house or apartment she roams, and how big the rooms are. Some ferrets will use the box 100 percent of the time. A rare ferret will make only sporadic visits. But, fortunately, most can be trained to use the box most of the time.

Litter box lowdown

To increase the odds of success, make sure that the bathroom facilities are adequate. Pay attention to the type of litter pan you buy. Ferrets back up into a corner and lift their tails before relieving themselves. If you pick a box with low sides, the mess will just drop over the side and

Pick a litter pan with high sides and a low entry.

onto the floor. What you need is a pan with high sides for backups, and a low entranceway for short legs. The litter boxes and pans made specially for ferrets fit the bill. Some cat pans may also be suitable—cut out a low entry if necessary. Because ferrets like privacy on the job boxes with hoods are a good choice as long as the doorway is ferret accessible. A ferret that can't get into her box easily will take the easy way out and plop elsewhere.

Some of the best litter boxes are homemade. Buy a plastic storage container or dish pan approximately 14-in. long × 10-in. wide × 7-in. high. To provide a low entrance, cut out a 4 × 4-in. section from one of the shorter ends. Be careful not to cut down too far, or you'll have more litter out of the box than in.

Ferrets are prolific poopers, so scoop out the waste once or twice daily. Wash the box weekly with plain soap and water or a nontoxic odor neutralizer like Critter Fresh. To keep the area around the box clean, tape plastic carpet runner to the floor underneath. Newspaper is acceptable too, if your ferret doesn't shred it or eat it.

Pick of the litter

No one litter is perfect for every ferret. There are pros and cons with each type, so weigh the differences and make the choice that's best for you and your pet. Your first consideration should be to find something

Newspaper keeps the floor clean under a homemade litter box.

that agrees with your ferret. Then consider your pocketbook, your environmental commitment, and your clean-up tolerance.

Regular clay cat litter suits many ferrets just fine. It's cheap and readily available, but dusty. A ferret tunneling through dusty litter can develop respiratory problems or eye irritation, so the ninety-nine percent dust-free litter is safer. Occasionally, the clay itself can cause skin and fur dryness, in which case a pelleted litter will be kinder to your pet.

Clumping litter is also inexpensive and easy to clean with a scoop. It's great if you have multiple boxes to clean. However, it might not appeal to meticulous housekeepers because it can be tracked through the house and is extremely difficult to remove from carpet fibers. The tiny particles can also get stuck to paws and bottom and ingested if your pet licks himself. Again, if dust irritates your pet's eyes or lungs, switch to a pelleted product.

Many experienced ferret owners recommend pelleted paper litter like

Yesterdays News or Kozy Korner Ferret Litter. Being made of recycled paper, it's a good environmental choice. It doesn't track through the house, it's dust free, it's absorbent, and odor control is good. But be aware that some ferrets will eat this litter and paper pellets can swell up, causing internal blockage.

Alfalfa-based green litter also comes in pellet form. Odor control is good, the litter isn't dusty, and it doesn't get carried onto the carpet. A comparable and inexpensive substitute is good old rabbit food. For maximum savings, buy it in bulk. Crushed corn cob is another plant-based litter, which has reasonable odor control and absorbency, but is bad for tracking. Again, watch that your ferret doesn't mistake these litters for lunch!

An excellent choice is Cat Works, a pelleted litter made from all-natural grain by-products. It is highly absorbent, unscented, biodegradable, has superior odor control, and is practically dust free. Few ferrets show any interest in eating it. But if your ferret tries a nibble, there's no need to worry. The pellets break down into minuscule pieces that won't cause a blockage.

Cedar shavings are *not* recommended for litter because they can cause respiratory problems in small animals. In fact, it's advisable to stay away from any wood shavings or chips. Shredded newspaper isn't a good option either. It doesn't absorb well, the ink can come off, and some ferrets eat it.

Whatever litter you choose, don't change from week to week with the sales. Your ferret might boycott her box if it contains something new. If you must change types, start by putting the new litter into the box and cover it with a layer of the old. Gradually increase the new and decrease the old until you've changed over completely. When switching litters, always keep a close eye on your ferret. If she starts eating or caching the new stuff, get rid of it.

When your ferret's ready to go, she'll back up into a corner with tail raised.

Cage training

When nature calls, ferrets back into a corner, lift their tails, and answer. Take advantage of this habit and place the litter box in a corner of the cage, ready to catch the droppings. The problem is that the potty pan won't stay in the corner long if your pet has her way. Many ferrets keep busy, busy, busy arranging and rearranging the contents of their cages. The litter box is a prime target, and your industrious scene shifter will pull, push, drag, and tip even the best of boxes. To keep it in the corner, anchor it to the cage. The litter box can be attached to the cage just as the dishes were on page 4. Or you can make holes in two sides of the box with a hot nail and wire it to the cage.

Now it's time to get down to business. You'll have a head start on litter training if your kit has come from a breeder or shop where a litter pan has been available to her from day one. She'll already have the right idea about that box in the corner. But, if you're starting from scratch, here's a handy hint. A ferret uses the litter pan within minutes of waking. So catch her after a snooze, when she's starting her backward wiggle, and deposit her in the box. She'll soon learn that's where she's supposed to go. If she doesn't catch on, or plays and sleeps in the litter, give the box that lived-in look. Put in some droppings along with a urine-soaked paper towel and sprinkle some litter on top. Then pop her into the pan for a good sniff around. When she uses the box, bring out the Ferretone! Each successful hit deserves a generous treat. She needs to get the message that going in the box equals a reward.

What's this? Your pet has found a different corner of the cage with more ferret appeal? It's much easier to place the box in her chosen corner than to fight about it. Ferrets can be stubborn and she'll always win. If you're still not having any luck, try partitioning off part of the cage so that she's left with only enough room for food, bedding, and box. She's not likely to soil her eating or sleeping area, so she won't have much option but to use the box. Try to catch her in the act and reward her. When she's visiting the box regularly, give her back her space.

House training

For most owners, cage training runs smoothly. But your kit won't always be confined to her cage so you'll have to work on litter training around the house at the same time. The job is not as easy when she's outside the cage running around, exploring, and having fun. With so many exciting distractions, her attention just won't be focused on the litter box.

You might think a pan in the cage is all that's needed. However, once your investigator is out and about, she won't be too anxious to trot back into her cage for a bathroom break. After all, the door to freedom could slam shut behind her. So it makes sense to have a box in her play area as well as a box in her cage.

Start your ferret's house training in the room where she's starting to explore the environment. Put a litter box in a convenient corner, prime it with poop, set her inside, and give her a treat. Whenever she makes a repeat visit, praise her warmly and repeat the reward. If, however, you find her backing into another corner with tail up high, this is your signal to hightail her into the pan. You might have to hold her there gently for a few seconds until she performs. Got a ferret with an attitude who insists on leaping out? Keep your eye on her until she backs up again, then whisk her into the box as often as necessary until the mission is accomplished. Or, if she's making repeated attempts in a different spot, take the hint—that's where she wants her bathroom, so move the box. Then for every successful visit, dish out a treat—a little bribery works miracles. Try to slip her the reward right after she's done her business and before she leaves the box. She needs all the encouragement she can get to hit the jackpot every time.

So far, so good. When there's only one room to worry about, most ferrets get the hang of things pretty quickly. The real challenge comes when your ferret starts to explore more of the house. There are corners galore! And, for reasons known only to ferrets, when they make the rounds of several rooms, they won't always bother going far to find a box. Is your ferret making regular deposits behind the living room sofa to avoid a long trek back to the kitchen? With a Lazy Daisy, it may be easier to clean another litter box than the carpet.

Accidents will happen

Even the best trained ferret can have accidents. If you catch the culprit in the act, a loud, firm "NO!" along with a loud hand clap will help as you cart her off to the nearest box. Never rub her nose in the mess and don't spank her—she won't understand. When you find her calling card in the corner, but she's fled the scene of the accident, discipline after the fact won't do a bit of good.

Is your ferret a repeat offender in a particular spot? Don't bother with spray repellents; they seldom work. A better solution is to scatter some dry food over the area. Ferrets will rarely go potty where there's food. Does your pet gobble down the food and poop in the spot anyway? It's not worth the aggravation to argue over it. Why not go with the flow and put another litter box there?

Your ferret might be absolutely wonderful about her litter box stops for weeks on end, and then, bingo!, little piles will appear here, there, and everywhere but in the box. What gives? A little ferret nose just might be out of joint. Have you been gone a lot lately? Have other pets been over to play? This backsliding is a ferret's way of saying, "I'll show you a thing or two—or three or four!" Don't take it personally. Give her a few extra cuddles, and she'll be back to normal in no time. Or she may be backsliding because she's miffed about the state of her box. Some ferrets prefer a scrupulously clean pan; others favor a slightly used one. If your ferret ignores her facilities, perhaps her housekeeping standards are different from yours. In cases where litter habits go totally out of whack or stools are abnormal, it's important to schedule a visit to the veterinarian.

Fortunately, accidents are not hard to clean up and don't smell bad. Messes can be picked up with a tissue. Urine needs to be blotted with paper towels. Wash the area thoroughly and spray with a pet urine neutralizer.

If you can't handle the occasional accident, or if you have acquired a ferret whose habits aren't the best, perhaps you need to train yourself rather than your ferret. Don't let her out of the cage until she's used the pan, and you'll be one step ahead. When she's out romping around, watch for that backup signal and rush her to the nearest box. Return her to the cage every half hour for a pit stop. And when she falls asleep, always put her back in the cage so that she'll be right beside the litter pan when she wakes up. If you are still having trouble, confining her activities to one room will help with damage control.

Repetition and reward

It helps to keep in mind that kits are babies, and miracles don't happen overnight. For both kits and older adoptees, patience and understanding are important. Don't yell, scream, or get frustrated. Do reward, reward, reward. Remember that most ferrets can be taught to use the litter box most of the time. So hang in there and, before you know it, your ferret will be minding her pees and poos.

Chapter Seven
Coming When Called

"I'm a calling youuuu . . ."

Many ferret owners don't realize that their pet can be taught to come when called by name. This is not just a trick. It's a useful skill that may come in handy if your ferret ever escapes or gets into the heating ducts by mistake (surely his mistake and not yours!).

Your kit will never respond to his name like a dog will. If you have a mental image of your ferret bounding up to you, sitting back on his haunches, thumping his tail on the floor, and waiting for a pat on the head, then you're barking up the wrong tree. Your furry friend won't snap to it for praise alone: It's a tasty tidbit that will bring him running. "No goodie, forget it!" is the ferret motto.

Choosing a reward

Treats serve a dual purpose. They're an enticement to get your ferret to do something in the first place and they're used as a reward *every time* he successfully does what you want. This last point is crucial.

You must have a food reward that your ferret will absolutely love—beg for—die for. Finding the perfect treat, however, may not be so simple. Some ferrets can be finicky eaters. It may take a while to find that special treat, a wholesome one he'll be crazy about.

Ferretone is your best bet for starters. It's not just that most ferrets like this vitamin supplement—it's also good for them. Adult ferrets can have three-quarters of a teaspoon per day; kits get one and a half teaspoons. The great thing about Ferretone, as opposed to other training rewards, is that the daily allowance goes a long way when metered out in drops throughout the day. You can dispense the Ferretone more easily if you put it into a plastic squeeze bottle or something similar. Ferretvite is an excellent alternative. The daily allowance will provide many rewards, and the taste rates the ferret seal of approval.

Linatone is another vitamin supplement that ferrets enjoy. This can be used in place of Ferretone or Ferretvite. However, the recommended dosage of Linatone is only three to five drops per day, not enough for repeated rewards in training. *Do not use Linatone along with Ferretone or Ferretvite on the same day or you'll overdose your ferret on vitamins.*

An unusual but effective reward is your ferret's fur ball medicine. You do use this as a preventive measure, don't you? Most ferrets love the stuff. Fur ball prevention medicine is usually given three times per week. Check with your veterinarian for the recommended dosage. However, make your pet work for this reward! To be effective, it needs to be gulped down at one sitting, not divided into dabs. And remember that you can use this only on the days your ferret is due to have it.

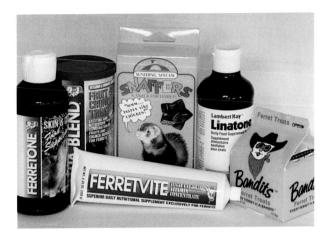

Tasty treats make training easier.

Family favorites for ferrets?

Has your ferret become fond of your favorite food? Does table food make a good treat? Cooked boneless chicken, beef, or fish can be given as often as your ferret wants without hazard to his health. Cooked meat is protein, and protein should compose a big part of your pet's diet. However, do not offer raw meat. It may contain harmful bacteria.

Other treats to try in moderation and in combination include raisin pieces, bits of green pepper or cucumber, smooth peanut butter, banana, watermelon, orange bits, celery, blueberries, apples, grapes, and any other fruit or vegetable. If anything on this list appeals to the little fellow, by all means use it as a reward. Your ferret will enjoy a change. But please, don't give him too much!

Tired of your pet nabbing your munchies? Now he can enjoy gourmet snacks of his own. A variety of delicious ferret treats are available from your pet shop shelves.

Treats, tasty but taboo

Picture this. It's Saturday night. A movie's in the VCR. You and your ferret are curled up on the sofa, dividing up the snacks—"A chip for you; a chip for me. A cookie for you; a cookie for me. Ice cream for you; ice cream for me." Wait! It's a great scenario, but these are treats to avoid. Ferrets don't properly digest sugars, dairy products, or carbohydrate-rich foods such as bread or pasta. Their intestines just don't process them.

No-no foods include red licorice (which most ferrets love), other candies, fruit-flavored or sugar-coated cereals, nuts, donuts, cookies, bread, cheese, chocolate, puddings, marshmallows, chips, popcorn, and dog biscuits. It's tempting to offer these foods because, just like you, your kit will love the very things he shouldn't have. But, for your ferret, it's not just a matter of keeping slim and trim. It's a matter of keeping healthy and free from intestinal problems.

The D-I-Y target stick

It takes just a few minutes to make this handy training aid—the target stick.

After you hit upon the gourmet treat that has your ferret drooling and licking his lips, you can start teaching him to love the sound of your voice calling his name. The first step is to make a target stick. What? You've never heard of such a thing? Well, now's your opportunity to learn

all about a useful and inexpensive training tool used by the pros.

It's really simple to make. Even those who hightail it fast at the very mention of do-it-yourself projects can make one of these in a matter of minutes. You need only three items—a piece of wooden dowel or stick approximately three feet long, a plastic spoon (the kind used on picnics), and some masking or duct tape. Tape the spoon onto one end of the stick so that the spoon becomes an extension of the stick. Picture the finished product as a spoon with a long handle—a very long handle.

Now, with treat ready and stick in hand, find your ferret and off you go. Oh, one more thing—be sure you've picked out a name!

It takes two to tango

Training your ferret to come when called is much easier if two people work together. Both people should sit on the floor about two feet apart. Person A holds the ferret, and Person B holds the target stick. Place a few drops of Ferretone on the spoon. Person B holds the spoon right under the student's nose and gives the command, "Bandit, come!" (Of course, if your ferret's name isn't Bandit, you should use his name instead.) The ferret's name should always come first, and the command must be the same every time.

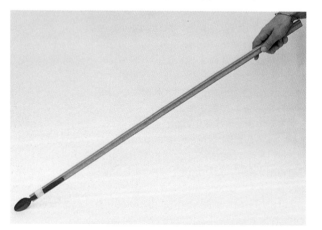

Be assertive when calling but use a cheerful, pleasant voice.

As the command is given by Person B, Person A releases Bandit making sure that he goes toward the stick. Constantly repeating the command, Person B gradually pulls the stick toward himself, enticing the pupil. In the best of circumstances, Bandit will actually follow the stick. When he reaches Person B, allow him to lick the Ferretone off the spoon as a reward. Give him plenty of praise for a job well done. Now repeat the process, with Person B guiding Bandit and Person A holding the stick.

Maintain this two-foot distance between Person A and Person B for a few days of practice until Bandit consistently reaches his goal. Increase the distance to two and a half feet for a few more days. Then gradually extend this span by six-inch increments. This may not seem like fast progress, but the small increments are necessary so that Bandit won't realize he's covering more ground.

When Person A and Person B get to be three and a half feet apart, and the stick is only three feet long, what happens? Person A with the stick puts the spoon under Bandit's nose and then backs up the required distance, all the while luring the little guy along. After one or two months of daily practice, it should be possible for Bandit to cover a distance of ten feet. Now's the time to stop putting the treat right under his nose. Instead, stand some distance

Person A on the right holds the ferret. Person B on the left puts the target stick under the ferret's nose.

Person B lures the ferret with a treat while calling his name.

The ferret reaches his goal and gets the reward.

away, show him the stick, and call his name. Bandit should have the hang of things by now and come running for the reward. Finally, dispense with the stick and go just to the spoon.

At this point, you can practice alone, experimenting with increasing distances. Be sure you're in Bandit's sight at first so that he can see the spoon. When he's got the knack, he'll come for any treat, from any room, whether you have the spoon or not.

Flying solo

So you don't have another family member or loyal friend who owes you big time? And you can't find someone to commit to three or four or five practice sessions daily? Worry not! You and Bandit can go it alone.

You still need to make a target stick. But, instead of a second person, what you need is a harness and leash. (See Chapter 9 for information on how to fit a harness and choose a leash.) The training procedure is the same as already discussed; the only difference is that you yourself guide your ferret. When you put the spoon under his nose and give the command, "Bandit, come!", gently pull on his leash so that he follows the stick as you draw it toward yourself. The leash prevents him from wandering away.

You have more control over your student when you use a leash, so it's very tempting to try longer distances sooner. Don't do it. Taking things in small stages, and repeating those steps frequently, is what ingrains the behavior. When do you get rid of the leash? That's a good question! When you reach the end of your rope (leash) and you see that Bandit's got the message, then it's time to let go.

Playing hooky

What happens when your kit isn't paying attention and wanders away? Try to avoid a runaway in the first place. But if he wanders even a smidgen, gently nab him before he makes the Great Escape and lead him right back to the stick. These sessions aren't playtime. Bandit has to know that this is school and not recess. If he runs away, bring him back to finish his homework.

There will be times when your pupil's so intent on his own pursuits that he actually ignores your calls. What do you do? The answer is simple—go after him. Get a little closer and remind him you've called. Don't let him get away with ignoring you. Always make sure Bandit finishes the task and always reward him.

Practice, practice, practice

Great ballet dancers practice hours every day, marathon runners train hours every day, concert pianists rehearse hours every day—not you and Bandit! You can accomplish great things with mere minutes of daily practice. Just how much is enough? Three to four short practice sessions a day are all it takes. Four five-minute sessions are much better than one twenty-minute session. Remember that a ferret has a short attention span on the best of days.

Don't hog the limelight. Let everyone in the household join in these practice sessions. Not only will it be fun, but your ferret will recognize the voices of everyone in the family and learn to respond to all of them.

Practice when perfect

So now your kit comes bounding with that little ferret dance every time you call—from the kitchen, from the dining room, and even from the

upstairs bedroom. Training him was easy, wasn't it? However, it's still important to reinforce his skills by daily practice, or as near daily as your busy life allows. It's also important to give a reward every time he comes. If you skip the treat, your ferret's smart enough to stop coming when you call him. Reward is important, now and two years down the road. As with other parts of his training, frequency and consistency are the things to bear in mind.

"Did somebody call my name?"

Chapter Eight
Hide and Squeak

Where's the ferret?

The kids are fighting in the hallway, waiting to get to school, you're already fifteen minutes late for work, and your furry friend is nowhere in sight. Tempers are fraying, your blood pressure's rising, and that darn ferret isn't coming when called. She's somewhere deep in dreamland. Does this scenario sound familiar? You *know* that little bundle of energy shouldn't run loose in the house while you're gone, but you can't wait around any longer.

Save yourself this aggravation. The next time you're out picking up pet food, check out the squeaky toys. It's a rare ferret who doesn't respond to one of these toys—immediately! Most will even rouse themselves from a sound sleep to answer the call.

Picking and choosing

Select your squeaky toy carefully. Many squeaky toys are available, but not all are suitable. What you're looking for is a stuffed toy with the squeaker hidden safely inside. Make sure that there are no pom-pom noses or plastic eyes that can be torn or ripped off. The squeaker itself should make a loud, high-pitched noise. Give them all a squeeze at the store to test them out. If you can, take your ferret with you. See what turns her on.

Pass right by the shelf with the cute rubber and latex toys. Your ferret will go crazy over these, but they're definitely on the danger list. If she gets her paws on one, or more likely her teeth, she could end up paying an unscheduled visit to the veterinarian.

Squeak and treat

After one squeak, most ferrets will automatically come running. Don't ask why; it just happens. The trick is to keep your pet coming to the squeak time after time. This is where rewards come in again! When she runs to the squeak, dole out a treat. Soon it'll be second nature—*squeak*–treat, *squeak*–treat, *squeak*–treat.

So, what can you do if your ferret's not a natural when it comes to a squeaky toy? It's rare, but it does happen. It's not a real problem; she can be taught what to do. Start by sitting in front of her with a treat. Make it a good one! Put the goodie under her nose and, as you squeak the toy, gradually entice her toward you. When she gets right to you, dole out the reward. Practice several times a day, gradually increasing the distance between you and your pet. You might find the target stick comes in handy here.

Soon you'll be able to stand in the kitchen (*squeak*), in the hallway (*squeak*), or in the bedroom (*squeak),* and your eager beaver will come running. She can even be snoring away, dead to the world, and she'll spring up and dash for her reward.

her little legs can carry her. Or, you might be tempted to use it too often. Don't overdo it. It's not a game. It's a way of getting your pet to surface when you need her.

When she answers the squeak, dish out a treat.

Knowing when to squeak

Your ferret's one smart cookie. If you squeak and treat only when you want to put her back into her cage, she'll soon figure out what you're up to and think twice about coming. So squeak for the good things in life too—kisses, cuddles, walks, romps—and she'll be sure to show up every time.

Because the toy works like magic (*squeak* and—presto—instant ferret), children might think it's great fun to *squeak, squeak, squeak* and watch their kit come scurrying as fast as

Crossed signals?

Occasionally, when you use the toy, you'll notice that your able student doesn't put two and two together. She hears the squeak. She rushes for the treat. The trouble is that she rushes to the wrong person. There you are squeaking away in the kitchen while someone in the hallway has a ferret dancing at his feet. What's the problem? Your ferret has a one-track mind—gimme that goodie! So, in her excitement, she accosts the first person she meets. To get her back on track, walk toward your baffled buddy and, when you're a few feet away, squeak again. She'll soon figure out who has the goods.

Lost and found

Indoors or out, a squeaky toy can be a lifesaver. If your ferret goes missing in the house, squeak in each room until she appears. If there's still no sign of her, she could be stuck somewhere. Squeak again and listen for her scrabbling. She may need to be rescued from a tight corner.

Should she escape from the house, get outside as soon as possible and squeak all over the neighborhood. If she's in earshot at all, she'll come for her treat. The squeaky toy is particularly helpful when a search party is out after dark. Even though you won't see her, she might hear you. And you might hear her if you keep your ears open for her bell.

Chapter Nine
Walking on a Leash

Take a walk on the wild side

That's exactly what you'll be doing if your ferret isn't properly trained to walk on a leash. He'll dart under, over, and in front of your feet. You'll be doing wild dances in the street to avoid stepping on the poor thing. You could even injure him if you misjudge your step. Dragging him down the street on a six-inch leash isn't the answer. Of course, you could always leave him home and forget the walks, but you don't have to give up. Just put him through his paces for a couple of weeks, and before you know it, you'll be parading proudly through the neighborhood.

A Lassie he won't be. Heeling, stopping, or staying on command won't ever be part of his repertoire. But he can learn to walk at your side without getting tangled up in your toes. When he's mastered the following techniques, be prepared for approving glances and admiring comments.

All kitted out

Before you hit the streets, you'll need to invest in a harness and a leash. Choosing a leash is easy. One that is lightweight nylon, three-eights inch wide and four feet long will do nicely. A swivel hook at the end is best. Check with your ferret about his color preference.

Because he might slip out of his collar and vanish, your pet must have a harness for walking. It's well worth your while to look for one of the excellent ferret harnesses on the market. Or you might find something suitable in kitten supplies. You need a harness that's easy to put on your ferret. It has to provide room for growth, but it must be a snug fit for your kit. How snug is snug? You should be able to get the tip of your baby finger, but no more, under the straps. If the harness is any tighter, you'll strangle him; if it's any looser, you'll lose him. For the perfect fit, try before you buy.

Remember that your ferret is very low to the ground. Any dangling

Getting the feel of things

If your kit fusses about wearing his new harness, do yourself a favor and don't bother putting it on until he's past the baby stage. It's not worth the fight. When he's a little older and more amenable to wearing one, he'll need to spend some time indoors getting used to it. Buckle him up a couple of times a day and let him run around for half an hour. You'll have fun watching him adjust to his new gear.

After a few days, attach the leash, hold on to it, and see how your kit reacts. He may not like it at first. In fact, he may even try to bite through it. A little perseverance and a few squirts of Bitter Apple on the leash will soon discourage him. The great advantage to starting indoors is that you can make sure his harness is tight enough to prevent escape before you face the great outdoors. Here's one more point—never leave your pet unattended while he's outside in his harness and leash, not even for a minute. He could be harmed or wiggle free.

Fit your ferret's harness so he's comfortable but can't slip out.

straps, which might trip him, should be trimmed, leaving an inch or two for growth. If the harness is nylon, hold the cut end to a lighted match. This will melt the end and stop it from fraying. Smooth any sharp edges while the nylon is still warm and pliable.

Right on target

Remember that invaluable piece of equipment, the target stick? Remember how you used it to teach your ferret to come when called? Well, now's the time to get it out again. To turn it into a dual-purpose stick, you'll have to add another piece. There's already a plastic spoon taped to one end. Take an identical spoon and tape it to the other end at a right angle to the stick. The finished product should look like a golf club. No, the stick isn't for putting practice!

Add another plastic spoon to your target stick, and you can start leash training.

On your mark, get set, go!

Now that the harness is properly fitted and your stick is ready, it's time to graduate to the outdoors. First, determine which side you want your ferret to walk on, right or left. Don't switch at your fancy—your ferret will only get confused. Choose whichever side is comfortable for you and stick with it. Most right-handed people prefer the left side, which is the traditional one for walking pets.

Start by taking the leash in your left hand. If necessary, shorten it up by wrapping it around your palm. This keeps your pet beside you so he can't wander from the straight and narrow. Prime the spoon with a few drops of Ferretone and take hold of the stick with your right hand.

The game plan is simple. Put the spoon directly in front of your ferret's nose, but just out of reach—tempting and tantalizing, close enough for him to see it and smell it, but not close enough to taste it. Walking slowly, with the stick held slightly ahead of him, coax your ferret along a dis-

tance of one foot. Then give him his reward. Beware of cheating—you'll be surprised how long his tongue is! Repeat the sequence several times, encouraging his efforts in a pleasant, firm voice, and that's enough for the first practice. As always, the more short practices you can work in per day, the better.

Maintain the one-foot distance for the next few days and then gradually increase the distance a foot at a time. Don't try to hurry the progress even if your ferret seems capable of going farther faster. It's frequent practices over short distances that will have your pet pounding the pavement in no time.

Start with the treat under your pet's nose . . .

. . . entice him to walk along by your side . . .

. . . a little farther yet . . .

. . . then give the reward.

Noise shy

Hoots, hollers, honks, slams, sirens, squeals, birds, barks, and backfires are just a few of the sudden sounds that might startle your buddy on your daily walks together. And on holidays or special occasions, what about firecrackers, noisemakers, and bursting balloons? If your ferret jumps suddenly, if his fur stands on end and he starts to scuttle backwards, you can be sure he's frightened. It's important to be aware that your pet can be scared easily by loud noises, especially if he's purchased in the winter and spends most of his first few months indoors. Crowds can also be scary. From a ferret's-eye view, all those feet look like a stampede. For safety in a crowd, use a carrier. (See Chapter 11.)

Don't keep yanking him along when he's scared. Gently scoop him up. Speak to him in a reassuring voice and soothe him by cuddling and petting. Carry him along for a while before you put him down again. As he has more frequent exposure to strange noises, he'll gradually become desensitized to them.

There are, however, some scaredy cats who never enjoy being outside. The sights and sounds are just too overwhelming. If, after a determined effort, you find that your ferret isn't enjoying the outdoors, don't force him. Give him his daily exercise indoors and avoid a lot of frustration for both of you.

Take the rough with the smooth

Introduce your ferret to a wide variety of surfaces—cool damp grass, loose gritty gravel, soft moist dirt, smooth hard pavement, rough uneven brick. That way he won't balk at changing terrain and will be much more versatile in where you can take him. Whatever the terrain, keep your eye on the ground. Did the neighbor's kid leave a balloon lying about or drop a rubber band? While you're walking with your head in the clouds, your ferret could be pouncing on unexpected treasures at your feet. If you frequently walk your pet on hard surfaces, he may require extra foot care. Pamper those paw pads. To prevent drying out and cracking, apply a moisturizer regularly. Whenever you put lotion on your hands, rub some into your ferret's feet!

Winter woes

There's a foot of snow outside, an icy blast greets you at the door, and your buddy is sitting there, leash in mouth, ready to go. Now what do you do? If the weather is extremely cold, it isn't reasonable to think about going outside for a walk. There are, however, a few options, whether your ferret is a novice or a seasoned leash walker. One is to go for a tour of your house or apartment. There's no reason why your ferret can't get some practice and/or

Try the park for a change of scene.

exercise walking from room to room. A basement, if you have one, makes an excellent indoor track. Another possibility is to bundle up you buddy and head for the nearest pet shop or pet supply store. Most managers don't object if you drop by to say hello and walk around the store. Wherever you do it, any indoor walking is better than no practice at all.

If, however, the winter weather is suitable for walking, there are some precautions to keep in mind. Because a house ferret isn't used to outside temperatures, your kit will need a warm sweater or coat. Finding one that fits properly may be tricky. Short ferret legs have a tendency to slide right out of the sleeves of most pet coats. Again, try before you buy.

A winter wonderland can be a perfect playground for your ferret. He'll love to slip, slide, and tunnel in the snow, clucking like crazy as he chases snowballs and snowflakes.

Just don't overdo it. Be careful that his feet don't get too cold or his fur too wet. When you bring him back inside after a winter romp, a brisk rub in a fluffy towel is better than a hot toddy! Sneezes and sniffles aren't restricted to two-footed walkers.

Cold temperatures aren't the only winter worry. Road and sidewalk salt can cause serious burns on your ferret's foot pads. Never allow your pet to walk on salted streets or sidewalks. And always wash off his feet after a winter stroll to remove any traces of salt or grit.

Summer sweats

Would you take a walk in the heat of summer, muffled from head to toe in a fur coat? Of course you wouldn't! Your ferret won't relish the idea either. If you're not careful, heat exhaustion can threaten your pet's life. In very warm weather it may be better to confine your walks to the early morning or the cool of the evening. Another good idea if you're out for long is to carry a freezer pack with you. Your ferret can lie on it to cool off. Use common sense in gauging how far your ferret can walk comfortably. If he shows *any* signs of discomfort while walking in the summer, get him out of the heat immediately.

For your ferret, a walk when it's warm may be like running a race. So carry a small bottle of fresh water on your summer strolls. Before your buddy starts to puff and pant, be sure to offer him periodic drinks. If he won't drink from the bottle or bottle cap, try getting him to lick the water from your finger.

Think of the last time you skipped across a parking lot or beach in the scorching summer heat with bare feet—ouch! Ferrets don't wear shoes and have no way of telling you that the sidewalk is hot. You have to be the judge of what's safe and comfortable for his tender tootsies.

After his walk, why not let him have a dip in his own private pool? A plastic dime store special is ideal. Many ferrets enjoy an occasional swim as long as the water isn't too cold. Forget the laps in the family pool, though. The chemicals aren't safe for him. He shouldn't take dips in the ocean, either. Swallowing salt water is hazardous to his health.

Patch skinny-dipping on a hot summer's day.

Keep off the grass

WARNING PESTICIDE USE—you must have seen these signs around your neighborhood. They are meant not only for people but also for pets. Think about how your ferret rolls and slithers through the grass, sniffing every blade. If the grass has just been sprayed with weed killer, pesticides, or fertilizer, then it isn't the grass your ferret should be playing in. The chemicals could be a health risk. So, if you see a sign indicating the recent use of toxic sprays, pick up your pet and walk elsewhere.

Other herbaceous hazards to avoid include poison ivy, cacti, and nettles. You'll know the plants to look out for in your part of the country. As a general rule, whatever you

should avoid, your ferret should avoid. Calamine lotion might be a fine remedy for people suffering from poison ivy, but it's a bit hard to get it through a thick coat of ferret fur!

Warning! This grass is harmful to ferrets, too.

Those pesky pests

Any furry pet walking outside has the chance of catching every pet owner's nightmare—fleas! Not only are these little bugs pesky for your kit, but they can also turn your carpeting into Fleatown overnight. Be constantly on the lookout for fleas when grooming your ferret. Before you spot any, you should check with your veterinarian for a recommended remedy to have handy for the inevitable attack. Cat flea shampoos are fine, but stay away from flea collars, dips, and dog products. Here's a homemade flea soap to try:

¼ cup Ivory or Palmolive dishwashing liquid
3 cups of water

Mix together and use as a shampoo. Avoid eyes. Leave the suds on your pet for three minutes. Rinse well.

Does the thought of even one flea have you scratching? Find out about flea prevention products such as Program or Advantage, which are available by prescription from your veterinarian. Although developed for dogs and cats, these products are often prescribed for ferrets.

Not only are mosquitoes a nuisance, but they can also infect your pet with heartworm. Ask your veterinarian whether this disease is prevalent in your area and, if so, ask him about preventive medicine. Does your ferret politely decline to swallow the stuff (yyuukk!) and spit it right back at you? A little bit of Ferretone makes the medicine go down. Just mix the required amount of medication together with a few drops of Ferretone, and he'll lap it up.

Scoop the poop

The last few paragraphs have all addressed environmental hazards that could affect your pet. However, the shoe will be on the other foot unless you carry a trusty pooper-scooper for cleanups. Be a responsible pet owner and take along a small plastic bag and some tissues for potty stops.

Beware of the dog

Be alert on your walks. Scan the horizon; look 'fore and aft. What you're watching for is trouble—in the shape of dogs, particularly the unleashed variety with no visible owner. Even dogs on a leash can pose a danger if they like to chase small furry creatures. When you see a leashed dog, cross the street or pick up your ferret and pass by at a distance. It's better to be safe than sorry.

Stray dogs are a more serious matter; there's no owner around to control them. If you round a corner and find yourself face to face with a roving runaway, don't assume the dog will go merrily on its way and ignore you both. Take immediate action to protect your ferret. Grab him and stuff him into your shirt, coat, or whatever to get him out of the dog's sight. Quickly put as much distance as possible between you and the stray. If it persists in following, make a beeline for the nearest neighbor, shop, or place of safety.

Where strays are a real problem, the best defense may be a good offense. An effective product to have in hand if you come eyeball to eyeball with a menacing mutt is a mild, dog-repellent, pepper spray. Letter carriers and joggers use this spray as protection against fierce canines. It's a humane deterrent, causing discomfort but no actual harm. Aim for the dog's face when you spray, making sure you and your ferret are out of range. Then beat a retreat. If this measure seems somewhat extreme, just remember that your ferret might look like lunch to a hungry stray. An aggressive dog that means business could pose a very real threat to you and your pet.

Cats are easier to deal with. If you find your ferret being stalked by a tenacious tabby, take offensive action. Pick up and protect your ferret and then scat that cat. Cats, dogs, and ferrets can get along together quite happily in the same house. It's unexpected encounters that spell trouble. The bottom line is—it's better never to take a chance with a strange dog or cat.

Strolling down the avenue

So now you and your ferret are part of the neighborhood scene. These walks with your buddy are bringing you double takes, eager questions, and new friends. They are giving him the opportunity for snooping, sniffing, romping, and rollicking. Enjoy your strolls together; take time to smell the roses. This is your reward for work well done!

Chapter Ten

Fun and Games

All work and no play

All work and no play makes Jill a dull girl! Because your ferret alternates between long hours of sleep and furious bursts of activity, play is important as an outlet for her energies. It gives her the exercise she needs and alleviates boredom. Playtime is just as important as formal training time. A ferret learns by playing. This is how she improves her social skills and finds out what's acceptable and what's not. Play develops trust and encourages bonding. Ferrets love to play—it's part of being a ferret.

People games

Playing with your ferret will bring out the kid in you. All the games you loved as a child are natural ferret fun. Take tag, for example. This is on the top-ten list. Chase your ferret around the house or apartment, gently tap her tail, and then encourage her to chase you. She'll soon pick up the idea, and you'll both be romping through the rooms, laughing and clucking.

Hide-and-seek is a big hit. Ferrets know instinctively how to play this game. When your rascal runs and hides under the sofa, go looking for her, calling out, "Jill, where are you?" Imitate her "dooking" sounds and announce, "Ready or not, here I come!" Act excited when you find her, and she'll happily run to another hiding place. Who cares if you look foolish?

Give peek-a-boo a try. When your ferret runs under the sofa or chair, gently tap at the bottom skirt. She'll stick her nose out and sniff. Sing, "Peek-a-boo!" as you *gently* rub her nose. Tap the skirt at a different spot. She'll scurry over to it and stick out the tip of her nose again. Surprisingly, she'll keep this up for quite a while, scooting from spot to spot as you tap.

Tug-of-war is another winner. This is an easy one. Hold one end of an old towel and give your ferret the other. She'll latch on immediately, pulling and tugging, trying to get it away from you. She'll swirl and roll around, grabbing with her paws, giving it her best shot. Be gentle, though—broken teeth are hard to fix. And watch out! After she gets the hang of this game, she might yank at anything that dangles— shirts on door knobs, sheets over the bed, towels in the bathroom. How's she to know the difference between the play towel and your best guest towel?

Another game ferrets can't resist is mock combat. It involves getting on the floor with your ferret and letting her pounce on your hand. Move your hand around and she'll chase it. Tickle her tummy and she'll jump up and pounce on your hand again. Now she's doing the ferret war dance—springing around, back hunched, fur bristled. No, she's not on the attack; she's just having fun. Be sure to keep this game playful. If it becomes too rough, it needs to stop.

While you and your ferret are engaged in mock combat, why not lob a few sock bombs? Gently toss balled-up socks in Jill's direction and watch her leap to intercept them. If you make your bed the battle ground, Jill can hide under cover between bomb attacks.

Ferret bowling will get your furball clucking for sure. The trick is to be *gentle* and *easy*. Find a laneway of smooth, polished floor space, cleared of all obstacles. Pick up and support your ferret with both hands. Point her posterior in the desired direction and, saying, "One, two, three!", send her sliding along the floor on her tummy. She'll come running back for more and more and more!

Bouncing balls

Ping-pong balls are great for starters. Bounce a few at a time on a hard floor and watch your pet go scuttling every which way. She'll grab a ball with her front paws, roll around and around, jump up, bat at the ball, and then chase it. For a change of pace, attach one to a string and swing it in front of her. Or, fill a box with ping-pong balls, toss her in, stand back and watch the dance. A ball or two in the cage helps beat boredom. They're safe as long as they're not dented. Throw any dented ones into a cup of boiling water to make them as good as new. Toss out any cracked ones.

Natural rope or sisal balls are a good choice, as are tennis balls, but golf balls might be a bit hard. Don't offer sponge, rubber, or super balls, please. Anything that could have a piece bitten off is off limits for your pet. Don't be discouraged if your little darling loses interest in her ball. Ferrets can be elated with a toy one minute and drop it abruptly the next.

Farley loves his ping-pong ball.

Just for ferrets

Toys geared just to ferrets are popping up all over. Ferret balls are large and hollow with holes for investigating. You can even buy colored plastic see-through tunnels that attach to the balls to make a maze. Tie a ferret chew bone to a shoe string and dangle it in front of your pet's nose. These bones are ferret tested and approved. In the cage or out, hammocks and trampolines, springy donuts, and hanging tubes will keep your ferret amused. Soft material tubes and tents can round out the playground.

More a toy for you is the large selection of fashionable ferret-wear. With hats, T-shirts, and bandannas, your pet can be the best-dressed ferret on the block! Don't forget her Halloween costume and Santa suit.

Spoil your pet with special ferret toys.

Filched from Fido, captured from Kitty

Why let Fido and Kitty have all the fun? Some dog and cat toys, such as Booda Bones, cat balls, and Cat Racket Sacks, are just the thing for ferrets. However, let the buyer beware! Some cat and dog toys are *not* suitable because they won't stand up to a ferret's roughhousing. Stay away from toys with feathers, buttons, pom-poms, leather, and rawhide. If it can be pulled off, bitten off, chewed off, or gnawed off, it's a sure bet your ferret will take it off.

Homemade treasures

Here's good news for ferret owners! Some of the best-loved, most enduring, and certainly cheapest play toys for ferrets are not store-bought at all. They're homemade treasures devised from everyday items you have on hand. The all-time favorite is a plastic shopping bag with the handles cut off—not a dry cleaning or bread bag. Your pet will spend hours (okay, minutes) rooting around inside the bag. She'll have double the fun if you join the game. Roll her around in the bag, drag her gently across the floor, and listen to her cluck. Better yet, bring out a pile of bags and let her dive right in. Warning! If you have a ferret who loves to eat plastic, these bags are not safe. Put a few ping-pong balls inside a paper bag instead and get the video camera out!

Do you have a large plastic milk or water jug headed for the recycling bin? Recycle it instead to your pet's toy box. Cut several holes in it and let your ferret's imagination do the rest. Do you have any plastic two-liter pop bottles? Cut off the tops and bottoms and then cover the sharp edges at both ends with masking or duct tape—instant tunnel fun! Cut the legs off old sweat pants or jeans—more tunnel fun!

Dig, dig, dig! Fun, fun, fun! A clean plastic garbage can with a lid makes a great ferret sandbox. Cut out a four-inch circle about eight inches up from the bottom of the can. Pour in four inches of sandbox sand or a mixture of sand and potting soil. It won't take long for your ferret to find the hole. Bury some balls for a treasure hunt. In the winter, try snow instead of sand.

Is that an empty shoe box? No, it's a new hidey hole. Tape down the top and cut a circular hole out of one end. Throw in a few ping-pong balls followed by the ferret. Ferret will clatter; balls will scatter.

Do you have a few bored kids hanging around? A box maze for the ferret is just the project for a rainy afternoon. Any combination of boxes will do—tissue boxes, cereal boxes, cracker boxes—the more the merrier.

Hammocks are great for sleep or play.

Packaged entertainment

What household doesn't have boxes, boxes, and more boxes lying around? Don't throw out that empty cereal box. It makes a handy ferret wagon. Punch a hole in one end of the box, reinforce it with tape, and attach a long shoe string. Let your ferret crawl inside and pull her around—free ferret transportation! Don't go too fast, though. You don't want a speeding ticket.

The ultimate ferret favorite

What's inexpensive, a snap to make, and at the top of the ferret favorite list? It's the terrific tube tunnel. Your ferret will love this toy because it gives her a chance to do what comes naturally—hide and tunnel. You'll love it because it's cheap, no tools are needed, and you can make it even if your fingers are all thumbs. Pick an afternoon or

evening when everything on TV is boring and trot down to your nearest building supply center for the following materials:

- four sections of plastic corrugated drainage tubing (also known as weeping tile). Each section should be two to three feet in length and four inches in diameter. Be sure to get the kind without the holes and have the sales clerk cut it to size.
- two elbow connectors.
- one T-connector.
- one piece of medium grade sandpaper. (Hey, this isn't a tool!)

When you get home with the goods, here's what you do.

- Smooth the rough edges of the cut tubing with the sandpaper.
- Snap tubing sections into connectors.

That's all there is to it. A few minutes work for you; hours of fun for your ferret. Everything can be easily taken apart and rearranged to give your pet a new challenge. As time and money permit, you can add more tubing and connectors to expand her subway system. For more crazy capers, try dangling a chewbone into the T-connector or throw in a few ping-pong balls.

Chapter Eleven

The Perfect Portable Pet

On the go

Ferrets love being around people. They also enjoy seeing the sights and exploring new places. What's a better way to do this than right along with you? As you go about your errands, picking up the mail, going to the library, and dropping off the dry cleaning, take your pet with you. His life will be more interesting when he meets people and goes places. And you'll enjoy his company. However, it's not always practical to haul him along with you on a leash; nor is it always safe—he could get stepped on in a crowd. For worry-free outings, a carry bag is often better for both of you.

Pouch your pet

The type of carry bag you choose is limited only by your imagination. The ones made just for ferrets are worth hunting for. These can double as sleep sacks, and they get a ferret five-star rating.

Some back packs are roomy enough for a hitchhiker. Try to find one that can be worn on your front where you can keep an eye on your passenger. Gym bags with shoulder straps and adequate ventilation are another possibility. Check your closet for shoulder bags, large purses, or cloth shopping bags. An infant snuggle sack with the leg openings stitched up will also work. If you like to sew, browse through the pattern books under crafts or accessories for something suitable. Or, take a piece of fleece-backed material approximately thirty inches by fifteen inches, fold it in half, and stitch up the side seams. Add a strap and you're all set. A pocket on the pouch is an added bonus. It's a perfect place to pack food, water, and walking leash. Remember that your ferret needs to eat and drink frequently, and your outings may take longer than planned. Take along a cold pack in the summer in case the weather turns hot.

Whatever you choose, make sure the carrier is sturdy and washable,

roomy and comfortable, with nothing rubber, plastic, or sponge hidden inside. Toss in a favorite blankie, and you're ready to go.

Jack-in-the-box

You pop him in, he jumps out. You pop him in again, he jumps out again. You'll never get anywhere this way! How do you persuade your pet to stay put? Never fear; it just takes a little indoor practice—and a little bribery. Whip out that Ferretone or his favorite goodie. Put him in his carrier and, as you stroll around the house, dole out tiny tidbits. Pat him on the head; tell him what a good boy he is. Every time he starts to struggle, say "NO!" in a firm voice and settle him back in the carrier with another bit of treat. Make the treat last so that he stays in the carrier for longer and longer periods. Pretty soon he'll enjoy his daily rides.

An ounce of prevention

Just in case your bold adventurer is tempted to bale out of his carry bag, a simple addition to it can prevent some anxious moments. A short, permanent leash inside the bag will keep him from escaping. This is especially helpful if your hands are full and he makes a bid for freedom.

Find a cheap, narrow kitten or dog leash with a swivel hook at one end. Make a mark on the leash twelve inches up from the hook and cut at this point. Pass a lighted match over the cut edge to stop any fraying. Sew this end to the inside of your ferret's carrier.

Where exactly in the carrier you attach the leash—top, bottom, or middle—depends on the type of bag you've chosen. What you're aiming for is to have the leash long enough to give your pet freedom of movement but not so long that he gets tangled up. If a twelve-inch leash is too long, shorten it a bit. A cheaper solution is to buy narrow polypropylene tape or rope (from the fabric store) and a small swivel hook (from the hardware store) and make your own leash. Whichever route you take, your next step is to put your pet in his harness, plop him in his carrier, and clip on the leash. Now when he tries to hop out, he won't get far.

Watch for the wiggles

Is your ferret trying his darndest to get out of his carry bag? He may have a legitimate reason. More often than not, persistent wiggles mean potty time. You'll have to get him out of the bag, clip on his regular leash and let him do his business. Have tissues and plastic bag in your pocket to clean up any mess.

Take me out to the ball game

You can take your pet almost anywhere—the hockey arena, the football stadium, the skating rink, or the soccer field. How about picnics, garage sales, outdoor concerts, antiquing, fishing, or hiking? The possibilities are endless when your pet is trained to a carry bag. Just don't make his first afternoon on the town too hectic. He could easily be overwhelmed and frightened by strange people and places. Introduce him to the social scene gradually. The idea is to socialize him, not to scare him.

Here's a word of advice. Your furball may be ready, willing, and able to go anywhere, but he won't be welcome everywhere. Be a responsible pet owner and check in advance. Never try smuggling him into places. There could be unpleasant consequences—anyway, it's embarrassing if you get caught.

A short leash attached to the carry bag will stop your ferret from bailing out.

Chapter Twelve
Have Ferret, Will Travel

Bon voyage!

Basically anywhere you go your ferret will love to tag along. You could probably use a little company on your jaunts around town. And for family visits and vacations, there's no need to bother the neighbors for pet-sitting. Take your ferret with you. Here are some tips that will help make your travels together safe and hassle free.

Public transit

Is public transit your main means of getting about? Check with your local transit office before taking your pet on busses, trolleys, street cars, or the subway. Different cities have different regulations. It's best to get the policy in writing. After all, the worker at the wicket may not have current ferret facts at her finger tips. Do you prefer taking a taxi? If so, phone the company before you hail a cab.

Always keep your pet in an escape-proof carry bag or travel carrier and show consideration for other passengers. A little ferret head poking out to say hello could cause pandemonium on the bus.

Short trips— buckle up

Do you usually get around in a car? Most ferrets are willing passengers. The very basic rule for car travel with a ferret is *never* allow her to wander loose in the car, *ever*. A free-roaming ferret can be a liability to herself, to you, and to others on the road. Think of what could happen if your pet decided to sniff at the brake pedal the moment you needed to stop. Even a parked car is not a good place for ferret rummaging. There are holes for hiding and sneaking, dangers lurking beneath the seats, odds and ends in the ashtray, and thingamajigs under the dash. In short, she has lots to get into.

How do you keep your pet in one place? For short trips around town, you can use a seat restraint. Buy a small coupler at your pet store. Put your ferret into her harness. Latch up the seat belt on the passenger side as if someone were sitting there. Wrap one end of the coupler around the seat belt once or twice. Then attach one of the snap hooks to the coupler's center ring and the other snap hook to your ferret's harness. If this makes the restraint too long, attach both hooks to the harness. This setup allows your frisky friend some freedom of movement, but keeps her in the seat. It is not, however, a safety device.

Before setting out in the car, wait until your pet has used her litter box. There's nothing more annoying than to be a mile from home and have your furball start that litter box dance.

Long hauls

Are you planning a vacation that involves a long car ride? If you can't bear to leave your baby at home, you need to prepare a bit differently for lengthy trips. First, the seat restraint won't do. How could your passenger get at her litter box, food, and water? For long hauls a travel carrier is the answer. There are many sizes and styles out there. Look for one that fits your car and your budget but is big enough for all your pet's paraphernalia. Some travel carriers are made to be used with a seat belt. This prevents them from flying through the air if the car stops suddenly. For others, loop the car seat belt over the top of the carrier, through the handle, and then buckle up. Is the seat belt too short? Buy an approved extension.

To keep your ferret in his seat, start with a coupler . . .

. . . latch the seat belt and wrap the coupler around it . . .

. . . hook up your ferret, and you're ready for the road.

When you're packing your own suitcase, don't forget to pack one for your ferret's gear. A lock-top plastic storage container, a small diaper bag, or anything similar will do. What should you take?

food for the trip
leash
Ferretone
squeaky toy
zip-lock bag of litter
plastic bags for droppings
fur ball medicine
nail clippers
a water bottle
harness
Bitter Apple
favorite toys
litter scoop
brush
carry bag
health documents

On the trip, an occasional ferret will drive you crazy scratching to get out of her travel carrier. To avoid this, make sure that your ferret's had ample opportunity to explore her portable cage before the journey, and get her used to car rides well before you travel any distance. She'll be more likely to fall asleep after a good workout, so tire her out before leaving home and let her stretch her legs whenever you stop to stretch your own. Ignore all her scratching, or she'll learn that scratching equals getting out. Most ferrets soon give up and snooze while you drive. If all else fails, turn the radio up louder (just joking!).

Temperature's rising

Some like it hot, but your ferret does not. In fact, high temperatures in a car during the spring, summer, or fall can be life threatening to your pet. Even a mild day with bright sunshine can turn a car interior into an oven in a matter of minutes.

Never put your ferret into a hot car. Cool it off first by running the air-conditioner for a few minutes. No air-conditioning? Try a blast of aerosol coolant made especially for reducing the car's interior temperature. You can tolerate much higher temperatures than your ferret can, so if your car doesn't have air-conditioning and you must transport your ferret in hot weather, try the following suggestions. Install a portable car fan that attaches to the dashboard and aim it at your buddy. Wrap hard-sided cold packs in towels or pillow cases and put them next to her. (Avoid the gel packs in plastic bags because your ferret

The travel carrier can be a home away from home with a favorite toy and bedding.

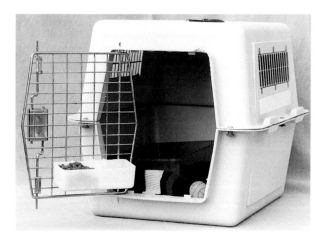

might tear the bag.) If you don't have any cold packs around, improvise! Freeze water in margarine tubs or plastic pop bottles. Put ice cubes in plastic food containers or zip-lock bags. Or, you can rig up a car window shade.

Frequent flyer

Is your pet going to be racking up frequent flyer miles? Better contact the airlines first. Some allow pets. Some do not. Some allow pets to be carried on board. Some do not. Ask in advance and get it in writing. You'd be furious if you got to the ticket counter and found out that no one has any idea whether the airline allows those *things* on board.

If your pet can fly with you, there are airline travel bags made just for the purpose—large enough for a small litter box, food, water, and your globe-trotter, but small enough to fit under the seat. Before leaving, call your veterinarian for advice on flying with your ferret.

Heartbreak hotel

It's late, you're looking for a motel, and every one has the *No Pets Allowed* sign hanging out front. Do yourself a favor when traveling with your pet—call ahead and make reservations. Otherwise, you might find that there's no room at the inn. Luckily, ferrets don't bark or whine in the middle of the night, so many

PATCH

motels will put out the welcome mat for your well-behaved pet.

Never let your ferret run loose in a motel room. Remember what a tireless explorer she is. Do you think the manager saw to the ferret-proofing before you arrived? Your ferret could easily get under the beds, rip a hole in the cover and get caught in the box springs. How do you explain this to the front desk? She could swallow a little something the cleaning staff missed, and your veterinarian is a thousand miles away. She could crawl under the dresser and refuse to come out at checkout time. No problem, you think? Just move the dresser and pull her out? That's fine, unless, of course, the furniture is fastened to the wall.

So you can't let her run loose in the room, and you certainly can't keep her confined in her cage the whole time. What's the answer? While at the motel, any playtime should be done on a leash, with the end tied to the travel carrier or held by you.

Your ferret needs a suitcase, too.

After a bedtime workout, Kalum's ready for a good night's sleep.

P.S. If you have to go out and leave your ferret in her cage, leave a reassuring note for the housekeeping staff.

The paper trail

Before you set off on your travels together, have all your ferret's documents on hand and up-to-date. Take along her health records, proof of rabies and distemper shots, and a current health certificate issued by an accredited veterinarian.

It's very important for you to know that certain states, cities, and small towns have declared themselves Ferret-Free Zones. Others have a variety of restrictions in force. The laws about these furry pets are so quirky and changeable, you should check the regulations before your journey. Are you planning to cross international borders? Call months in advance and ask for information in writing. Import permits may be necessary to take your gadabout across borders or to get her back home.

If you thought scratching was annoying in the car, you'll appreciate it even less in the middle of the night when you want to sleep and your ferret wants to explore. Don't wait until the scratching starts; there's a lot you can do to prevent it. After you've settled into your room, put your pet on her leash and let her snoop around. She can satisfy her curiosity under your watchful eye; then she'll be less likely to bug you at 2:00 A.M. Wear her out before bedtime with a brisk walk and energetic play. March her up and down the corridors; she'll enjoy patrolling the halls. Just look out for foreign objects that could wind up as a midnight snack. If she gets a good enough workout, she'll be glad to get into her cage for some shut-eye. To minimize any disturbance when you're sleeping, park her cage in the bathroom, close the door, and find your earplugs.

If you want a warm welcome

Don't take your pet along uninvited. Please ask first. Just because you love your ferret doesn't mean that Uncle Ray and Aunt Margie will, even if you've named your darling after one of them!

Chapter Thirteen
Sitting Pretty

Smile for the camera

Is it family portrait time? If you want your ferret to sit up and smile for the camera, you'll have to teach him how. Well, maybe not the smiling part, but he can be taught to sit. And it's pretty easy. In fact, it's probably the easiest training so far. Of course, he won't sit on command like a dog. You can say, "Patch, sit!" until you're blue in the face, and he'll go on his merry way regardless. But grab those ferret treats, read on, and you'll have your ferret "sitting pretty" in no time.

Trick for treat

Striking a picture-perfect pose comes naturally to most ferrets. They just don't *know* they can do it. That's where you come in. First, clear the decks for action so that your pet's not distracted. Then pick

Sitting up is easy to teach. Put a treat by your ferret's nose . . .

. . . gradually raise the treat so he sits up to get it . . .

. . . then give a reward.

one of his favorite treats. Put it right in front of his nose and say, "Patch, sit!" Raise the treat up, tempting him to follow it until he's sitting on his haunches. Then give him the reward and lots of praise. Don't let him cheat! He's wily enough to try leaning on the nearest chair, cupboard, or knee. Or, he might try grabbing the goodie. Repeat this three or four times at a "sitting", several times a day.

again. Get a special one ready and perch your ferret comfortably on your shoulder. While you walk around the house, let him nibble or lick the tidbit from your finger. Be careful, though! Don't let him fall or jump off. The goal is to keep him on your shoulder for progressively longer periods of time. Talk softly to your pet and stroke his head. After he gets the hang of things, he should be happy to ride there without putting a dent in the treat supply.

Hitching a ride

Are those little legs tired? Are you halfway home from the park and your buddy needs a break? Hitching a ride on your shoulder could be the answer. Some ferrets have no trouble with a balancing act. Others, however, need a bit of encouragement. So, it's good old treat time

No head for heights?

Do you have a scaredy cat who doesn't appreciate a bird's-eye view? He might feel safer on your shoulder if you start by sitting rather than standing. Or, you might try waiting until he's a little older and not quite so frisky. Speaking of frisky, if he's really squirmy, it may be litter box time.

Some ferrets are just not shoulder sitters. If yours falls into this category, don't force him. Try the front pouch of a sweatshirt instead. It's better to have a happy ferret than a hurt ferret.

Hood-winks

That scaredy cat who won't sit on your shoulder might be happy to hole up in the hood of your sweatshirt or coat. This is another popular means of ferret transportation. Training to a hood can be a little more difficult than to the shoulder. The technique is the same, but, because you don't have eyes in the back of your

head, it's hard to know what your baby's up to. Beware of a bail out! Another pair of hands could be helpful during training to prevent a fall. Once he's happily hunkered down in your hood, he'll most likely catch forty winks.

. . . and hitching a ride in his hood.

Chapter Fourteen

Stay Out of Those Houseplants

Green thumbs beware

For all you houseplant aficionados (and who isn't?), here's a word of warning—ferrets love wet soil. With just one whiff of that delectable aroma, damp earth, your furry friend will be off and running—where's the plant, where's the plant, where's the plant? And when she reaches her goal, will your ferret be content to smell the flowers or admire the foliage? Not on your life! For your ferret, pay dirt means play dirt.

Ferrets love to dig and tunnel. Your houseplants provide a convenient outlet for this obsession. Apart from the mess digging can cause, it can be detrimental to the health of your plants. Even worse, some plants can be hazardous to the health of your ferret. If your kit gets into a dieffenbachia, for example, she could be poisoned. Stinky's owner spent hundreds of dollars in veterinary bills after his determined digger dug in a dieffenbachia.

On page 65 is a list of the more common plants that can be toxic to house pets. If you have any of these plants, put them well out of your ferret's reach. It's always better to play it safe.

Soil-saving solutions

There are a number of possible solutions to the houseplant dilemma. The following suggestions have all been proven effective. However, not every suggestion will work for every ferret. You'll have to experiment to find out what works for your pet.

The simplest strategy is to sprinkle a thick layer of black pepper directly onto the soil in the plant pot. Ferrets are no more partial to black pepper up the nose than people are. Another variation on this solution is to mix citrus peel (lemon, lime, or orange) into the soil. These are items you probably have on your kitchen shelves already.

Hazardous Plants

acalypha
ageratum
allamanda
amaryllis
anthurium
aucuba
autumn crocus
azalea
bird-of-paradise
boxwood
browallia
brunfelsia
burro's tail
calla lily
castor bean
Chinese evergreen
clivia
croton

cyclamen
dieffenbachia
elephant ear
English ivy
eucalyptus
euphorbia
heliotrope
holly
honeysuckle
hoya
hyacinth
hydrangea
iris
jasmine
Jerusalem cherry
lantana
lily of the valley
mistletoe

narcissus
natal palm
oleander
ornamental pepper
petunia
philodendron
poinsettia
primrose
pyracantha
sago palm
senecio
spider plant
star jasmine
sweet pea
Swiss cheese plant
tulip
wax begonia

The next suggestion relies on repellent smells. Scent-off pellets for dogs and/or cats can be purchased at most pet shops, pet supply stores, garden centers, and some hardware stores. To use these pellets safely and to keep your ferret from trying a sample snack, you need to put them into a container such as a baby food jar. Poke a few holes in the lid, place some pellets in the jar, and tightly secure the lid to the jar with masking or duct tape. Place the container on top of the plant dirt. The smell of the pellets will escape through the holes and discourage your ferret from taking pot shots at your plant. You can try the same technique with moth balls or crystals (the smelly kind). Never

sprinkle Scent-off pellets or moth balls directly onto the plant dirt. Ferrets have been known to eat things that aren't good for them.

For the home herbalist, here's a concoction that's worth a try. (It will also keep cats out of your garden and your spouse at bay.) In a spray bottle, mix the following:

1 tablespoon of cayenne pepper
2 tablespoons of garlic powder
2 cups of very warm water

Shake well and spray the soil, the bottom leaves, and the top of the planter. You'll need to repeat the spraying every few days and certainly after watering the plant. All it takes is one sniff, and most ferrets

*Wire mesh
and landscape
stones keep
plants safe
from ferret
attacks.*

will head off in the opposite direction. The only slight glitch is that it can repel family members as well! Success with this method might depend upon the level of garlic tolerance in your household or on the number of plants you have.

Bitter Apple spray is worth a try, too. Spritz some around your plants just as you did the garlic spray. Some ferrets won't be deterred by this product because they like to play in the dirt, not eat it. For other ferrets, the smell of the Bitter Apple is enough to curb their earth-moving maneuvers.

Do you have a squirt gun or spray bottle handy? If you're quick on the draw and can hit a moving target, a shot of water and a loud, firm "NO!" might stop your ferret in her tracks. However, it's difficult to catch her in the act each and every time. And some ferrets think this is a game.

If all else fails

As a last resort, there is one sure-fire solution that will work for larger pots. Fit overlapping pieces of galvanized half-inch mesh screening on top of the plant dirt, trimming it to fit with wire cutters. Don't waste your money buying regular window screening that your ferret can easily rip with her claws. Next, cover the screening with landscape stones, two to three inches in diameter. Make the layer of stones at least two inches thick. As an inexpensive alternative, try flat river rocks. Your ferret

*Oh, no!
Foiled again!*

will have difficulty moving the larger landscape stones or rocks. However, if you have a little Amazon, the screening will prevent her from hitting pay dirt. With some plants, the use of screening may not be feasible. In this case, pile up those larger stones as deeply as possible. Where the pot is too small for stones, or if it can be easily knocked over, find a sunny spot well out of ferret reach.

A loud, firm "NO!" is in order whenever the little digger goes near a plant—every time . . . always. Consistency is the key. She needs to know you mean business.

The greenhouse effect

If you try these suggestions, your plants can come down from the ceiling hooks and onto the floor again.

You won't have to sell them off at your next garage sale. Once more, your home can be a green oasis. And you can keep the ferret, too.

"Where's the plant, where's the plant, where's the plant?"

Chapter Fifteen

Don't Sweep the Carpet Problem Under the Rug

An itch to scratch?

Carpet clawing by your favorite fuzzy is not only very annoying, but it can be quite destructive as well. If your ferret gets obsessive about scratching a certain carpeted corner, you could end up with hardwood floors in no time.

Why do some ferrets *scrraaattchh* at carpets? There are usually two reasons. First, the little rug rat probably wants into a room you have designated off limits. When Chester wants to explore behind a closed

Scratching to get in?

door, you can guarantee he'll try to tunnel his way to the other side. This is bad news for your carpet. The second reason for clawing is that Chester wants under something, be it the sofa, the chair, or the TV stand. Ignoring the problem won't make it go away—and a ferret should never be declawed—so here are a few solutions to try.

Redirect that scratch

Every time Chester starts to scratch the carpet, pick him up quickly, say "NO!" loudly and firmly, and move him from the area. The best place to plunk him is at his very own scratching post or plank. This redirects his negative behavior (carpet clawing) to positive behavior (scratching the post). Be certain, however, that you don't buy your ferret a carpet-covered scratching post or he'll have trouble distinguishing between the carpet that's okay to claw and the carpet that isn't. Instead, find a post covered in sisal rope—the more tightly wound, the better.

Get a whiff of this

Some ferrets don't like the smell of Bitter Apple spray, let alone the taste. Because you already have this spray around, it doesn't hurt to use it. Spray a little bit on an inconspicuous spot of carpet to test for color fastness; then spray it on the area Chester likes to claw. You'll need to respray the area twice a day so that the smell doesn't dissipate, but don't saturate the carpet. If you're lucky, your ferret will take one sniff and run the other way. Will dog and cat spray repellents work? They won't work for most ferrets.

Cover up

Short of posting a sentry at the doorway, you may never be able to stop your ferret's scratching. But, you can at least protect the carpet from damage. Purchase a length of plastic carpet runner, cut it to fit the threshold exactly, and place it nubby-side down. All four sides need to be taped to the floor with wide masking or clear packing tape. Don't miss even a fraction of an inch or the great investigator will find the gap and wiggle under the plastic. Now, when Chester tries to attack the broadloom, he'll scratch the runner, not the rug. The plastic may even discourage his clawing completely.

Tape down a plastic runner and protect the carpet.

Ferrets are, however, crafty little creatures. If they can't scratch their way *under* the door, watch them try scratching their way *through* the door. Door scratching is annoying, destructive, and difficult to stop. Try covering the lower part of the door— the part he can reach—with a piece(s) of smooth plastic runner. Tape all four edges securely to the door. If there are any small breaks in the tape, he'll be able to rip everything off. A smear of Bitter Apple spray or cream on the plastic will prevent him from tearing at it with his teeth. Whenever you do catch him storming the door, say "NO!" and scoot him to the scratching post. What happens when you're too late and he's already made his mark? Painted doors can easily be retouched, and any scratches in stained woodwork can be camouflaged with brown shoe polish or liquid scratch cover.

Doorways aren't the only place you may find Chester digging. After you've ferret-proofed the sofa, he

A Scat Mat (Pet Mat) protects both floor and door.

aid, recognized by humane societies and veterinary associations, that will keep your pet away from a particular spot when nothing else will. When using it with ferrets, remove and throw away the rubber feet from the bottom of the power pack. Place the mat wherever Chester's raking your rugs and secure it with masking or clear packing tape. When he walks on the mat, he'll be surprised by a tingling sensation similar to static. It's quite harmless but gets the message across—keep off!

may have lingering memories of his cozy nest underneath. Months later, he'll still be scratching to worm his way in. Discourage him by using plastic, tape, and spray, as outlined previously, or use a Scat Mat.

SCAT!

Scat Mat, also marketed as Pet Mat, can be found at your local pet supply store. It's an effective training

Carpet shark

Does your ferret love to glide through the carpet, nose first? Don't use powdered carpet deodorizers or cleaners. These can irritate little chins, eyes, noses, and lungs. So scrap these powders and let your ferret surf safely through the rug like a true carpet shark!

Chapter Sixteen
Odds 'n' Ends

Company's coming

Are friends coming for the weekend? When a ferret's part of your family, you'll have to worry about more than the menu and the sleeping arrangements. Every guest visit is a golden opportunity for your busybody. She'll be quick to take advantage of a door left open, a cupboard ajar, a bag lying on the floor. Any open suitcase will be an open invitation to snoop. Your ferret's not particular. She'll steal from the guests just as happily as she does from you. Cosmetic sponges, slippers, mittens, kid's toys, baby supplies, medication—the list of possibilities goes on and on.

New toes could be a tempting new target for your ferret to nibble. So when you're bringing out the drinks, why not bring out the Bitter Apple, too, and ferret-proof those exposed toes? And visitors don't think about watching their step, so make sure that they don't step on your ferret. For safety's sake, she may have to spend more time in her cage. The bottom line is—be alert when company comes. And be considerate. You may love your little cutie, but your company may not appreciate ferret kisses.

Cache and carry

Or is it carry and cache? Caching is an instinct in ferrets. You can't really control this behavior. No matter what you do, the little pack rat will keep stashing away stolen treasures. You'll be surprised what can wind up in her secret collection—remote controls, pliers, toys, can coolers, hair brushes, extension cords. Have you misplaced your keys? Check your ferret's stockpile. Does she do a hit and run on her food bowl—grab a mouthful and speed off to her hoard? Just make sure the food hidden in her personal pantry doesn't go moldy.

Ho! Ho! Ho! HELP!

Christmas is loads of fun for a ferret. Look at it from her point of view. You've just put out all sorts of wonderful new toys—the stockings at the fireplace, the table decorations, the swagged garlands on the banister, your heirloom nativity scene, and

Protect your tree— and, more importantly, your ferret— with a Scat Mat.

floor with tape, or the little sneak will tunnel her way under and hit those presents pronto. Remove any low-trailing branches, or she'll be smart enough to use one as a bridge over the mat. Does the idea of using a Scat Mat ruffle your feathers? Just remember that it's much better for your pet to experience a slight, harmless tingle than to have a tree crash down around her ears.

Tips

The following tips are not really training hints, but they could help make life easier with your ferret. Are you having trouble cleaning ears or cutting nails? A few drops of Ferretone on her tummy will keep your pet occupied while you take care of business. Most ferrets love to have their ears rubbed, so sneak in a cleaning while you massage. Or, try to do the grooming when she's fast asleep.

During the twice-yearly coat change, shedding can be controlled by using a small-toothed flea comb or a grooming mitt. Or, pluck your pal. Holding her over a newspaper, quickly tug out little bits of fur from all over her body. This is a fast and effective way to remove shedding hair, and it won't hurt your ferret one bit.

Does your ferret stubbornly clamp her jaws shut when it's time for medicine? Mix it with a little Ferretone or Ferretvite, and she'll lap it right up.

your number-one holiday headache with a ferret, the Christmas tree.

A real Christmas tree is just an overgrown houseplant to your pet— only better! There's the damp, earthy smell, sticky sap, water to drink, and branches to climb. An artificial tree is just as bad. It also has balls to swat, tinsel to steal, light cords to test, and piles of presents underneath.

The easiest solution for a no-hassle Christmas is to keep the room with the tree off limits for the holiday season. If that isn't possible, tie the tree to something sturdy close by, use only plain water in the stand, cut off all low-hanging branches, hang ornaments and tinsel well out of fer-ret reach, rub Bitter Apple cream on light cords, and keep presents locked away until the big day.

Or, if you like your tree the way it was last year, use a Scat Mat. A cir-cular or semicircular Scat Mat around the base of the tree will pro-tect it right through the twelve days of Christmas. Secure the mat to the

Screen savers

Window screens keep the bugs outside, but there's no guarantee they'll keep your fuzzy friend inside. For most ferrets, it's a breeze to knock out or scratch through a screen. This can lead to escape or injury—ferrets don't always look before they leap. Since there are no pet-proof screens, there are no easy answers. But here are a few suggestions: keep the problem windows closed, attach Plexiglas across the lower part of the screen frame, or use a Scat Mat (see Chapter 15).

Lost ferret

Ferrets are always looking for adventure and, even if you're very careful, escapes can happen. If your ferret slips away, organize a search party immediately and then get outside and squeak that squeaky toy all over your yard. No luck? Place her cage outside with fresh food and water. Fluff up her bedding and lay a trail of Ferretone drops to the cage. Check with neighbors; then fan out and squeak around the neighborhood. Still no luck? Call the Humane Society and ferret organizations in your area, nail up flyers and posters as quickly as possible, and check the lost-and-found services offered by your local newspaper and radio stations.

If your ferret's wearing a collar, bell, and identification tag, anyone finding her will know she's a pet, and you'll have a much better chance of a speedy reunion. But a runaway ferret will often ditch her collar, so microchip identification should be done at an early age as an added safeguard. Check with your veterinarian about this painless procedure.

Chapter Seventeen
Reaping Your Reward

Top of the class

Now your ferret has graduated from training, hopefully with honors! Your hard work has paid off, and the instruction time has been minimal when you consider the benefits. Gone are the days of chasing your kit out of the cupboards or the houseplants. Now you can devote your energies to having fun together. You won't have to waste time anymore searching under beds, in closets, or behind furniture for a mislaid pet. Instead, you can have instant ferret by calling his name or squeaking for him. No longer will you have to leave him home alone or bother Auntie Barbara to pet sit. He's now the perfect traveling companion.

Continuing education

Training is an ongoing job; you don't want your student backsliding after all your good work together. So always keep up the reminders and the rewards. In the end, it's your commitment and dedication that will give your ferret the opportunity to become the best pet he can be . . . and that is a pretty wonderful pet!

Useful Addresses and Literature

Ferret organizations and shelters

American Ferret Association
P.O. Box 255
Crownsville, Maryland 21032-0255
phone: 1-888-FERRET1
(1-888-337-7381)

Ferret Advice and Information
Resource (F.A.I.R.)
P.O. Box 952
Westmont, Illinois 60559
phone: (630) 968-8142

Ferret Family Services
P.O. Box 186
Manhattan, Kansas 66505-0186
phone: (785) 456-8337

Ferret Fanciers Club
2916 Perrysville Avenue
Pittsburgh, Pennsylvania 15214
phone: (412) 322-1161

Ferret Information Rescue Shelter
& Trust Society
FIRST (Ferret) Society
#113-3495 Cambie Street
Vancouver, British Columbia
V5Z 4R3
phone: (604) 263-7481
email: first@ferrets.org

League of Independent Ferret
Enthusiasts (L.I.F.E.)
P.O. Box 11007
Burke, Virginia 22009-1007

Legion of Super Ferrets (LOS)
P.O. Box 866
Levittown, Pennsylvania 19058-0866
phone: (215) 946-2747
fax: (215) 946-1291
email: pcflospa@aol.com

North American Ferret Association
P.O. Box 1963
Dale City, Virginia 22193-1963
phone: (703) 590-2132
fax: (703) 730-5131

Ottawa Ferret Association
Ottawa, Ontario
phone: (613) 258-6134

Shelters That Adopt and Rescue
Ferrets (STAR)
P.O. Box 1714
Springfield, Virginia 22151-0714
Please send a SASE for information.
email: STARFerret@aol.com

United Ferret Organization
P.O. Box 606
6 Water Street
Assonet, Massachusetts 02702
phone: (508) 644-5562
fax: (508) 644-5201

There are literally hundreds of local clubs and associations throughout the world. Check with any of these organizations to find one near you. And don't forget the abandoned ferrets looking for a good home. The shelters listed here can put you in touch with a shelter near you.

Books

The Pet Ferret Owner's Manual
Dr. Judith Bell
Miracle Workers, 1995
P.O. Box 68
North Rose, New York 14516

A Practical Guide to Ferret Care
Deborah Jeans
Ferrets, Inc., 1996
P.O. Box 450099
Miami, Florida 33245-0099
phone: 1-800-988-0988
fax: (305) 285-6963

Ferrets—A Complete Pet Owner's Manual
Chuck and Fox Morton
Barron's Educational Series, Inc., 1995
250 Wireless Boulevard
Hauppauge, New York 11788-3917

The Complete Book of Ferrets
Val Porter and Nicholas Brown
D&M Publications, 1997
Bedford, England

*The Ferret, An Owner's Guide to a
    Happy Healthy Pet*
Mary Shefferman
Howell Book House, Simon &
    Schuster/MacMillan Publishing,
    1996
1633 Broadway
New York, New York 10019

Ferrets in Your Home
Dr. Wendy Winstead
T.F.H. Publications, 1990
1 T.F.H. Plaza
Third and Union Avenues
Neptune City, New Jersey 07753

Periodicals

Ferrets USA (annual)
Ferrets (bimonthly)
Fancy Publications
P.O. Box 6050
Mission Viejo, California 92690
phone: (714) 855-8822

Modern Ferret
P.O. Box 338
Massapequa Park, New York
    11762-0338

Index

*F*un-loving
*E*nergetic
*R*ambunctious
*R*ewarding
*E*ndearing
*T*rainable